Target
Get back on track

GR 5

Edexcel GCSE (9–1)
Combined Science

Christine Boyd, Pauline Lowrie,
Ali Mclachlan, Katherine Pate,
Helen Sayers, Frank Sochacki

PEARSON

Published by Pearson Education Limited, 80 Strand, London, WC2R 0RL.

www.pearsonschoolsandfecolleges.co.uk

Copies of official specifications for all Pearson qualifications may be found on the website: qualifications.pearson.com

Text and illustrations © Pearson Education Ltd 2017
Typeset and illustrated by Tech-Set Ltd, Gateshead
Produced by Haremi Ltd

The rights of Christine Boyd, Pauline Lowrie, Ali Mclachlan, Katherine Pate, Helen Sayers, Frank Sochacki to be identified as authors of this work have been asserted by them in accordance with the Copyright, Designs and Patents Act 1988.

First published 2017

20 19 18 17
10 9 8 7 6 5 4 3 2 1

British Library Cataloguing in Publication Data
A catalogue record for this book is available from the British Library

ISBN 978 0435 18902 0

Acknowledgements
The author and publisher would like to thank the following individuals and organisations for permission to reproduce photographs:

Science Photo Library Ltd: Dr Gopal Murti 46; Alamy Stock Photo: Science History Images 48

Note from the publisher
Pearson has robust editorial processes, including answer and fact checks, to ensure the accuracy of the content in this publication, and every effort is made to ensure this publication is free of errors. We are, however, only human, and occasionally errors do occur. Pearson is not liable for any misunderstandings that arise as a result of errors in this publication, but it is our priority to ensure that the content is accurate. If you spot an error, please do contact us at resourcescorrections@pearson.com so we can make sure it is corrected.

This workbook has been developed using the Pearson Progression Map and Scale for Science.

To find out more about the Progression Scale for Science and to see how it relates to indicative GCSE (9–1) grades go to www.pearsonschools.co.uk/ProgressionServices

Helping you to formulate grade predictions, apply interventions and track progress.

Any reference to indicative grades in the Pearson Target Workbooks and Pearson Progression Services is not to be used as an accurate indicator of how a student will be awarded a grade for their GCSE exams.

You have told us that mapping the Steps from the Pearson Progression Maps to indicative grades will make it simpler for you to accumulate the evidence to formulate your own grade predictions, apply any interventions and track student progress. We're really excited about this work and its potential for helping teachers and students. It is, however, important to understand that this mapping is for guidance only to support teachers' own predictions of progress and is not an accurate predictor of grades.

Our Pearson Progression Scale is criterion referenced. If a student can perform a task or demonstrate a skill, we say they are working at a certain Step according to the criteria. Teachers can mark assessments and issue results with reference to these criteria which do not depend on the wider cohort in any given year. For GCSE exams however, all Awarding Organisations set the grade boundaries with reference to the strength of the cohort in any given year. For more information about how this works please visit: https://qualifications.pearson.com/en/support/support-topics/results-certification/understanding-marks-and-grades.html/Teacher

Contents

① Diffusion, osmosis and active transport

This unit will help you to understand how different substances pass through the cell membrane to get into cells or to leave cells.

This unit will help you to recognise and describe diffusion, osmosis and active transport.

In the exam, you will be asked to tackle questions such as the one below.

Exam-style question

1 All living cells must exchange substances with their environment. To enter or leave cells these substances must cross the cell membrane. Substances can cross the cell membrane in three ways:

diffusion, osmosis or active transport.

(a) Complete the table below to describe how these substances enter or leave the cell.

Substance entering or leaving the cell	How the substance crosses the cell membrane
Minerals entering a plant root from the soil	Active transport
Oxygen entering a liver cell	diffusion
Water entering a plant root from the soil	Osmosis + diffusion
Glucose taken up from the small intestine	Active transport

(4 marks)

You will already have done some work on this topic. Before starting the **skills boosts**, rate your confidence in understanding the three ways in which substances cross the cell membrane. Colour in ✎ the bars.

1 How do I know when diffusion will occur?

2 How do I know when osmosis will occur?

3 How do I know when active transport will occur?

The movement of liquids and gases into and out of cells can be described by **diffusion, osmosis** and **active transport**. Each process depends upon differences in concentration to influence the movement of molecules.

Molecules are always moving. They move from an area of high concentration to an area of low concentration. This evens out the concentration and is called **diffusion.** Diffusion is a **passive** process, which means it does **not** require energy to make it happen.

① Draw an arrow 🖉 on diagram 1 to show where the molecules will move.

Diagram 1

Osmosis is a form of diffusion to do with movement of water from high concentration to low concentration. It is also **passive** (requiring no energy), and it happens across a **partially permeable** membrane such as a cell membrane. This membrane works like a sieve allowing small molecules (like water) to pass through but not larger molecules (like salt or glucose).

② In diagram 2, which molecules can pass through the membrane? 🖉 ......_water_..................

Diagram 2

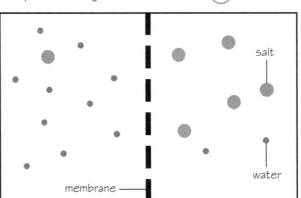

Look at the size of the molecules and the size of the holes in the membrane.

Remember In osmosis only the water molecules move through the membrane. A dilute solution has more water molecules so they will move through the membrane to the concentrated solution, where there are fewer. This is the only way to make the two solutions the same concentration.

③ In the diagram in **②**, what will happen to the concentration of salt molecules on the right of the membrane as water enters that part of the solution?

Water molecules will move through the membrane until the concentration of salt molecules is the same on both sides of the membrane.

Circle Ⓐ the best answer.

| stays the same | concentration rises | (concentration falls) |

Sometimes molecules need to move from a low concentration to a high concentration. This is known as **active transport** because this process requires **energy** from respiration.

④ Which of these diagrams illustrates active transport? Circle Ⓐ the correct letter.

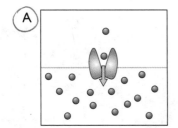
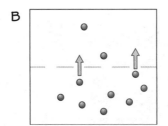
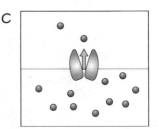

How do I know when diffusion will occur?

Remember that diffusion is the movement of molecules from where they are more concentrated to where they are less concentrated. This means the molecules become evenly spread out.

(1) Which diagram represents diffusion?
Circle (A) the correct letter.

Oxygen and carbon dioxide can easily diffuse across a cell membrane.

Oxygen is used inside cells during respiration. Therefore, oxygen will be at a low concentration inside cells.

Carbon dioxide is made during respiration. Therefore, the concentration of carbon dioxide inside cells is often high.

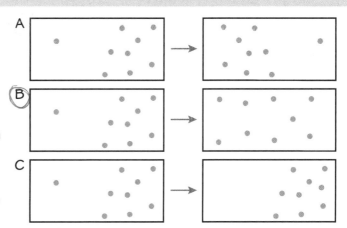

Answer ✐ this exam-style question.

Exam-style question

1   The diagram shows molecules of oxygen and carbon dioxide in solution.

   Both types of molecules can pass through the cell membrane.

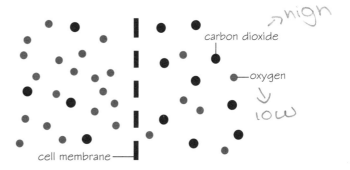

(a) State which side of the diagram shows a higher concentration of oxygen.

   left

   (1 mark)

(b) State which side of the diagram shows the inside of the cell.

   Remember This is where the carbon dioxide is made during respiration.

   right

   (1 mark)

(c) In which direction(s) will the molecules diffuse?

   ☐   A   Both to the right

   ☐   B   Both to the left

   Remember Diffusion occurs *down* the concentration gradient.

   ☐   C   Oxygen to the left and carbon dioxide to the right

   ☒   D   Carbon dioxide to the left and oxygen to the right

   (1 mark)

(d) Explain why oxygen will diffuse in the direction you have stated.

   'Explain' means that you must say *why* it happens.

   It diffuses down the concentration gradient. Oxygen will diffuse from right to left

   (2 marks)

Oxygen and carbon dioxide will always diffuse into and out of cells down their concentration gradients.

Biology

② How do I know when osmosis will occur?

Osmosis is a special form of diffusion. Osmosis is the diffusion of water molecules through a partially permeable membrane.

less water

- The water molecules move from a dilute (less concentrated) solution to a more concentrated solution.
- A dilute solution has more water in it than a concentrated solution.
- So water diffuses from where there are more water molecules to where there are fewer water molecules.

① In an osmosis practical the mass of four potato slices was recorded and they were placed in four different solutions for 24 hours. The mass of each one after 24 hours was then recorded again. The results are shown in the table below.

Distilled water   10% sucrose   20% sucrose   30% sucrose

Any question that asks about osmosis will be about the movement of water into or out of cells.

Solution	Distilled	10% sucrose	20% sucrose	30% sucrose
Initial mass (g)	10	10	10	10
Final mass (g)	11	10	9	8

a Calculate the % change in mass of each of the potato slices.

$$\text{Percentage change} = \frac{\text{actual change}}{\text{original amount}} \times 100$$

	Distilled	10% sucrose	20% sucrose	30% sucrose
Change in mass (g) = final mass − initial mass	change in mass = 11 − 10 = 1	10 − 10 = 0	9 − 10 = − 1	(8 − 10) = -2g
% change in mass = $\frac{\text{change in mass}}{\text{initial mass}} \times 100$	$\frac{1}{10} \times 100$ = 10%	$\frac{0}{10} \times 100$ = 0%	$\frac{-1}{10} \times 100$ = −10%	$\frac{-2}{10} \times 100$ = -0.2 × 100 = -20%

b Which piece gained mass?

A positive percentage change is an increase in mass. A negative percentage change is a decrease in mass.

_____ Distilled _____

c Explain the reason for the 10% sucrose solution result.

_____ It doesn't change same concentration inside the potato cell _____

d Why is using % change in mass a more useful measurement than change in mass in grams?

_____ You can compare them _____

③ How do I know when active transport will occur?

Active transport is different from both diffusion and osmosis. It uses **energy** from respiration in the cell and **transporter proteins** in the membrane to transport molecules across **against** their concentration gradient.

The diagram shows how active transport of a molecule occurs.

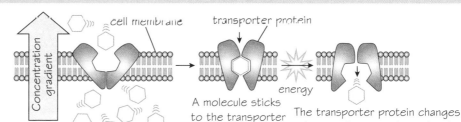

cell membrane   transporter protein

A molecule sticks to the transporter protein.

The transporter protein changes shape and carries the molecule across the cell membrane.

energy

Concentration gradient

① Complete 🖉 the paragraph using information from the diagram.

Active transport uses a _transporter_ _protein_ in the membrane.

A molecule fits into the protein and _energy_ is needed to carry the molecule

across the membrane. The molecule moves _against_ the concentration gradient.

② Complete the following table. Place a tick ✓ or a cross ✗ in every box. This will give you a useful summary about diffusion, osmosis and active transport.

Transport process	Molecules move down the concentration gradient?	Uses energy from respiration?	Molecules move against the concentration gradient?
Diffusion	✓	✗	✗
Osmosis	✓	✗	✗
Active transport	✗	✓	✓

Exam-style question

1 The table shows the changes in concentration of glucose along the small intestine after a pasta meal.

All the glucose is absorbed from the small intestine into the blood.

Distance from stomach (cm)	Concentration of glucose (mmol/dm³)
0	0
200	400
400	500
600	200
800	0

(a) Using information from the table, explain how we know that all the glucose is absorbed.

Look at the data for concentration.

It begins and ends with 0. **(1 mark)**

(b) Glucose is absorbed by active transport. Explain how active transport can make the concentration of glucose fall to zero between 600 and 800 cm along the intestine.

You are told this is active transport. How is active transport different from diffusion?

goes from low to high concentration and it uses energy. It moves against the concentration gradient. **(3 marks)**

Biology

Sample response

You could be asked to apply your knowledge of the processes by which substances enter and leave living cells.

Look at this exam-style question and the answers given by a student.

Exam-style question

1 The table shows a student's observations on the effect of growing radish seedlings in different types of water.

Water provided	Average height of seedlings after five days (cm)	Observations
Tap water	8.2	Growing well
Sea water	4	All plants have shrivelled and died
Distilled water (contains no minerals)	5.1	Yellowish leaves
Boiled and cooled tap water (contains no oxygen)	7.5	I thought these would die

(a) Explain the results observed for sea water.

All the plants have shrivelled and died. (2 marks)

(b) Suggest an explanation for why the plants did not grow well with distilled water.

There were no mineral ions in the water. (2 marks)

(c) Before the experiment it was predicted that the seedlings grown in boiled and cooled water would die because they had no oxygen. Explain how the seedling roots might have gained oxygen.

The oxygen diffused in and was used for respiration. (2 marks)

1 a Why is the response to (a) incorrect? *Look at the command word*

It says 'explain' not 'state'

b What process involving substances entering and leaving cells is being tested in (a)? *This is about the movement of water into and out of cells.*

Osmosis

c What would be a better response to (a)? *Think about the size of the molecules and the type of membrane.*

there is more water inside the roots, so it is moving from high to low concentration, semi permiable

2 Describe how mineral ions are taken in by plants and how they are used.

Active transport uses mineral ions to make protiens

Your turn!

Now use what you have learned to answer this question. Read the question thoroughly, looking for clues and apply your knowledge from other areas of biology.

Answer ✏ the exam-style question using the guided steps below.

Exam-style question

1   All living cells must exchange substances with their environment. To enter or leave cells these substances must cross the cell membrane. Substances can cross the cell membrane in three ways:

diffusion, osmosis or **active transport**.

water

Complete the table below to describe how these substances enter or leave the cell.

Look at the command word 'describe'. This means some detail is required.

Substance entering or leaving cell	How the substance crosses the cell membrane	
Minerals entering a plant root from the soil ↳ low concentration	the Minerals will enter the plant root using active transport. → Against the concentration gradient root hair cells → high concentration → requires energy (mitochondria)	You must draw on your knowledge from other areas of the syllabus. You will need to know that the concentration of minerals in the soil is lower than inside the plant cells.
Oxygen entering a liver cell ↳ low concentration → down the concentration gradient	→ diffusion → high concentration in blood → passive (energy not required)	Oxygen is used inside cells. Therefore, oxygen is at a low concentration inside the liver cell.
Water entering a plant root from the soil Osmosis diffusion	cytoplasm (osmosis) semi - permable membrane cell wall (diffusion)	Any question that asks about the movement of water into or out of cells will be asking about osmosis.
Glucose taken up from the small intestine	→ glucose goes into cells and respires (travells by the blood) → Then the glucose molecules that are left use active transport as there is a low concentration in the small intestine	Glucose is a useful nutrient, therefore all of the glucose in food is taken up into the cells of the small intestine.

(4 marks)

Need more practice?

You could be questioned about a practical you have carried out such as osmosis in potatoes.

Have a go at this exam-style question.

Exam-style question

1   A student investigated the movement of water into and out of potato tissue. This was his method:

dilute solution to the potato cell.

1   Cut five potato sticks that are each 5 cm long.

2   Calculate the mass of each potato stick and place in separate boiling tubes.

3   Place each potato stick into sugar solutions at different concentrations.   *lost water*

4   Leave overnight then recalculate the mass of each potato stick.

The student's results are shown in the table.   *lost mass*

Concentration of sugar solution (mol)	First mass of potato stick (g)	Final mass of potato stick (g)	Change in mass of potato stick (g)	Change in mass of potato stick (%)
1.00	1.85	1.65	−0.2	−10 %
0.75	1.70	1.58	−0.12	−7 %
0.50	1.80	1.70	−0.10	−5 %
0.25	1.96	1.91	−0.05	−2.55 %
0.00	1.76	1.87	0.11	6.25 %

change in mass / Initial mass x100

(a)   Complete the blank column to improve the validity of the student's results.   **(2 marks)**

(b)   Explain why the potato chip gained mass at sugar concentration of 0.00.

   0.00 is pure water. The potato has higher concentration compared to it's surroundings. by osmosis.   **(3 marks)**

Boost your grade

To improve your grade, make sure you know these main examples:

- Diffusion of gases in the lungs and diffusion of urea out of the liver.
- Osmosis investigation using potato slices and a range of salt or sugar concentrations.
- Active transport of minerals into plant root cells and of glucose into the cells of the small intestine.

How confident do you feel about each of these **skills?** Colour in the bars.

1   How do I know when diffusion will occur?

2   How do I know when osmosis will occur?

3   How do I know when active transport will occur?

② Enzymes

This unit will help you to understand how enzymes work to speed up biological reactions and what factors affect the speed of enzyme-controlled reactions.

In the exam, you will be expected to tackle questions such as the one below.

Exam-style question

1   A student investigated the effect of pH on the activity of an enzyme that digests starch.

The student recorded how long it took for all the starch to be digested.
The results are shown in the table.

pH	2	5	7	9
Time for complete digestion in seconds		305.0	180.0	280.0
Rate of reaction (s^{-1})	0	0.33	0.55	0.36

(a)   Describe how changing the pH affects the rate of this reaction.

.... (3 marks)

(b)   State the pH that gave the fastest reaction.

.... (1 mark)

(c)   Explain why the reaction was fastest at this pH.

.... (2 marks)

(d)   No time was recorded for pH 2. This is because the starch was not digested.

Explain why the enzyme was unable to digest the starch at pH 2.

.... (2 marks)

You will already have done some work on enzymes. Before starting the **skills boosts**, rate your confidence in each area. Colour in 🖉 the bars.

❶ How can I describe the action of enzymes?	❷ How can I explain the action of enzymes?	❸ How can I explain the effects of the conditions on enzyme action?

Biology

Enzymes are biological **catalysts** that speed up the rate of reactions. They are essential for all the reactions in the body. To understand how enzymes work you need to think about:

- the shapes of the individual molecules
- how their shape is affected by the surrounding conditions.

The substances that enzymes work on are called **substrates**. The substances that are produced are called **products**. Enzymes are always specific, which means that an enzyme will work with only one molecule (its substrate). The shape of the substrate molecule matches the shape of the enzyme. They fit together a bit like two pieces in a jigsaw puzzle.

1 The diagram shows an enzyme and four possible substrates.

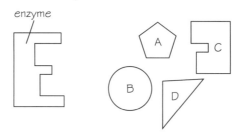

a Circle Ⓐ the substrate molecule that will fit the enzyme.

b Highlight 🖉 the space next to the enzyme where the substrate molecule will fit.

The substrate fits into the **active site** of the enzyme. The way the shapes of the enzyme and the substrate fit together perfectly is described as the **lock-and-key model**.

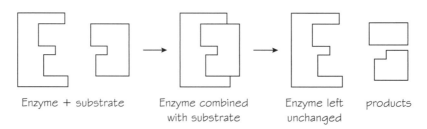

Enzyme + substrate   Enzyme combined   Enzyme left   products
with substrate   unchanged

Remember A catalyst is a substance that speeds up the rate of a reaction without itself being used up.

High temperatures and **extremes of pH** affect the shape of the enzyme's active site.

2 The diagram below shows the shape of the same enzyme after it has been boiled.

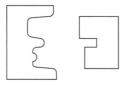

Circle Ⓐ the best word from the choice of bold words, to complete these sentences.

High temperatures and extremes of pH change the shape of the **substrate** / **active site**.

This means the substrate will not **fit** / **collide**. We say that the enzyme has become

reformed / **denatured**.

How can I describe the action of enzymes?

To describe the action of an enzyme, you need to state clearly what effect the enzyme has on the reaction. If you are given data, you need to look for a trend and describe it, using values to support your description.

① The table shows some data about the rate of an enzyme-catalysed reaction.

Temperature (°C)	Rate of reaction (in grams of product formed per minute)
20	7
30	39
40	54
50	32
60	11

a Circle Ⓐ the correct words in these sentences.   First you have to look at the effect of the enzyme.

> The enzyme breaks down the **substrate** / **product**. The more **substrate** / **product**
>
> formed per minute, the **slower** / **faster** the rate of reaction.

b Use the data in the table to complete the sentences.   Then look at the data and describe the trends. Use values to support the description.

> As the temperature increases from ....°C to ....°C, the rate of reaction increases.
>
> The reaction is fastest at ....°C. As the temperature increases to ....°C, the rate of
>
> reaction decreases.

② A student placed 10 cm³ of a protein suspension into a test tube and added 1 cm³ of a protein-digesting enzyme. The student measured the concentration of amino acids in the tube every 5 minutes. The graph shows the results.

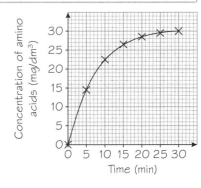

a What is the substrate? Underline Ⓐ it in the question.

b What is the product? Highlight ✏ it in the question.

c Describe ✏ what is happening in the reaction.

....

....

d What is the shape of the line on the graph? Tick ✓ the box that gives the best description.

Stays level with no change	☐
Rises slowly at first then rises more steeply	☐
Rises steeply at first, then more slowly and then levels off	☐

Look at the shape of the curve. This shows you the trend in the data.

e Describe ✏ the trend, using the description you have chosen in **d** and data values from the graph.

Give the values where the shape of the graph changes.

As time increases, ...

....

Biology

2 How can I explain the action of enzymes?

For a reaction to take place, the enzyme and the substrate molecules must collide. When the concentration is higher, there are more molecules. When there are more molecules, there are more collisions. When there are more collisions, the rate of reaction is increased.

① Look at this table of results.

Substrate concentration (mol/dm³)	0	0.5	1.0	1.5	2.0
Rate of reaction (mg/s)	0	3	6	9	12

Think carefully about the number of molecules of substrate and how often collisions will occur.

a When is the rate of reaction highest? Circle Ⓐ the substrate concentration in the table.

b Explain 🖉 why the rate of reaction is highest at this point by completing these sentences.

When the substrate concentration is zero ....

....

As the substrate concentration increases ....

....

The highest number of collisions is when ....

....

② The table below shows a range of conditions (A, B, C and D) in which reactions can occur. Condition C is present at the start of the reaction.

	A	B	C	D
Concentration of enzyme	high	low	high	low
Concentration of substrate	low	low	high	high

Remember that the **enzyme** will be left unchanged by the reaction, but the number of **substrate** molecules decreases during the reaction.

Circle Ⓐ the correct letter to answer these questions.

a Which conditions will cause the molecules to collide most often?   A   B   C   D

b Which conditions are found at the end of a reaction?   A   B   C   D

③ The enzyme amylase converts starch (the substrate) to maltose. The graph shows how the concentration of the product maltose changes during the reaction.

In each question, think about the number of molecules of starch.

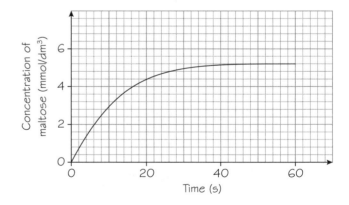

a Explain 🖉 why the reaction has stopped at 60 s.

....

b Explain 🖉 why the reaction slows down between 20 s and 40 s.

....

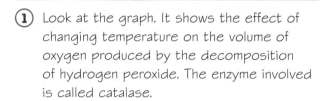

3 **How can I explain the effects of the conditions on enzyme action?**

At higher temperatures, molecules have more energy and are more likely to collide. Enzymes have an optimum temperature and pH at which they work most quickly. Extremes of pH or high temperatures can affect the shape of the active site, so that the enzyme becomes denatured and no longer catalyses the reaction.

1 Look at the graph. It shows the effect of changing temperature on the volume of oxygen produced by the decomposition of hydrogen peroxide. The enzyme involved is called catalase.

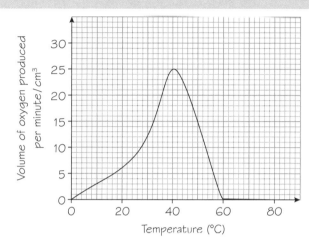

First check you understand the reaction.

a In the question above, circle Ⓐ the substrate and underline A the product.

b Circle Ⓐ the correct words.

> At low temperature (5 °C) the molecules have **lots of** / **very little**
>
> energy, so the molecules will be moving **very quickly** / **very slowly**.
>
> At this temperature the molecules will collide and react
>
> **very often** / **not very often**.

To explain the shape of the graph you need to think about the movement of the molecules.

c Complete ✎ the sentences.

Molecules are always moving. The higher the temperature, the faster they move.

- At higher temperatures (40 °C) molecules have .... energy.

- At 40 °C molecules will collide and react .... than at 5 °C.

d At what temperature is the volume of oxygen collected highest? Circle Ⓐ the best answer.

The **optimum** condition is where the enzyme works most quickly.

> 0 °C   10 °C   20 °C   30 °C   40 °C   50 °C   60 °C   70 °C

e What happens to the volume of oxygen collected as the temperature is increased above 60 °C? ✎

....

f Explain ✎ what has happened to the enzyme above 60 °C. What happens to the shape of the active site if the temperature rises too high?

....

....

....

Biology

Sample response

A good explanation about enzyme activity should:
- include key terms such as 'active site'
- refer to values from a graph or table if you are asked to interpret data
- explain rates of reaction in terms of numbers of molecules and collisions
- explain the effect of pH and temperature in terms of enzyme shape.

Look at this exam-style question and the answers given by a student.

Exam-style question

1 A student investigated the digestion of fat by lipase.

(a) Name the substrate and the enzyme.
The substrate is fat and the enzyme is lipase.
(2 marks)

(b) The student expected the reaction to be most rapid at the start of the experiment.

Explain why the reaction should be fastest at the start.
This is when the concentration of fat molecules is highest.
(3 marks)

The student altered the temperature and measured the rate of reaction at each temperature. The student plotted the results on the graph.

(c) Give the optimum temperature of the lipase enzyme.
40 °C
(1 mark)

(d) Explain why the reaction occurs most quickly at this temperature.
At low temperature the rate is very low, it gets higher as the temperature rises then falls again above 50 °C.
(3 marks)

(1) The student only got one mark for his answer to (b). What else should the student have included to complete the explanation?

Remember that enzyme molecules and fat molecules must collide for a reaction to occur.

(2) Use the graph to check the student's answer to (c). What is the correct answer?

(3) The student got no marks for his answer to (d). Write your own answer to (d) on a separate piece of paper.

Look at the command word.

What happens as the temperature increases towards the optimum?
What happens when the temperature increases further?

Your turn!

It is now time to use what you have learned to answer this exam-style question.

Remember to read the question thoroughly, looking for clues.

Make good use of your knowledge from other areas of biology.

Exam-style question

1 A student investigated the effect of pH on the activity of an enzyme that digests starch.
The student recorded how long it took for all the starch to be digested.
The results are shown in the table.

pH	2	5	7	9
Time for complete digestion in seconds		305.0	180.0	280.0
Rate of reaction (s^{-1})	0	0.33	0.55	0.36

(a) Describe how changing the pH affects the rate of this reaction.   You are asked to 'describe' not to 'explain'.

....

....   **Remember** In the exam you can write on the question paper. On the table write 'high' where the reaction is fast and 'low' where the reaction is slow.

....

....

(3 marks)

(b) State the pH that gave the fastest reaction.

....

(1 mark)

(c) Explain why the reaction was fastest at this pH.

....   Use the word 'because' in your answer. Most questions about enzymes need the words 'active site' in the answer.

....

....

(2 marks)

(d) No time was recorded for pH 2. This is because the starch was not digested.
Explain why the enzyme was unable to digest the starch at pH 2.   **Remember** When the pH is a long way from the optimum, the enzyme's active site is altered.

....

....

....

(2 marks)

Use this checklist to check ✓ your answers.

Checklist In my answer do I ...	✓
include key terms such as 'active site'?	
refer to values from a graph or table if asked to interpret data?	
explain rates of reaction in terms of numbers of molecules and collisions?	
explain the effect of pH and temperature in terms of enzyme shape?	

Biology

Need more practice?

In the exam, questions about enzymes could occur as:
- simple standalone questions
- part of a question on how cells, tissues and organs work in plants and animals
- part of a question about a practical test.

Have a go at this exam-style question.

Exam-style question

1   Enzymes are often called biological catalysts.

(a)   State what a catalyst is. ....

....

(1 mark)

Samples of the enzyme amylase were heated to different temperatures and mixed with starch. The rates of reaction were measured and then plotted on the graph.

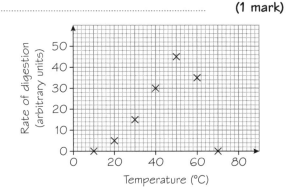

(b)   Draw a curved line through all the points on the graph.   (1 mark)

(c)   Estimate the rate of starch digestion at 35 °C.

....

(2 marks)

(d)   The rate of digestion at 70 °C is lower than the rate at 50 °C. Explain why.

....

....

....

(2 marks)

Boost your grade

You need to know about the enzymes carbohydrase (also known as amylase), protease and lipase and their substrates. You will also need to be able to calculate rates of reaction from data in a graph.

How confident do you feel about each of these **skills?** Colour in the bars.

1 How can I describe the action of enzymes?

2 How can I explain the action of enzymes?

3 How can I explain the effects of the conditions on enzyme action?

③ Cell division

This unit will help you to recognise when cells divide by mitosis and when they divide by meiosis. It will also help you to understand the importance of cell division in the cell cycle.

In the exam you will be asked to tackle questions such as the one below.

Exam-style question

1   Mitosis and meiosis are types of cell division.

(a)   Complete the table to show which of the features are produced by mitosis and which are produced by meiosis.

Feature	Mitosis or meiosis?
Production of egg cells	
A lizard growing a new tail	
Production of pollen in a flower	
Cells replaced on the skin to heal a cut	

(4 marks)

(b)   Name the organs that produce gametes (sex cells) in a man and in a woman.

A man ....

A woman ....   (2 marks)

(c)   Describe two differences between mitosis and meiosis.

....   (2 marks)

You will already have done some work on mitosis and meiosis. Before starting the **skills boosts**, rate your confidence in each area. Colour in 🖉 the bars.

1 How can I identify the stages in the cell cycle?

2 How can I describe situations where mitosis is occurring?

3 How can I explain the importance of meiosis?

Cells divide in a series of stages called the **cell cycle**. First, a cell grows larger and makes more sub-cellular structures like mitochondria (for energy production) and ribosomes (for making proteins). The cell then copies its chromosomes during **interphase**. **Mitosis** then takes place in which two cells are produced from one. One copy of each chromosome moves to each end of the cell, and the nucleus divides. The cell then divides into two new cells.

1 Number these statements (1-3) in the order in which they occur in the cell cycle.

Stage	Correct order
The cell increases in size and increases the number of sub-cellular structures such as ribosomes and mitochondria. DNA replicates to form two copies of each chromosome.	
The cytoplasm and cell membrane divide to form two identical, daughter cells.	
A set of chromosomes moves to each end of the cell and the nucleus divides.	

Human body cells have 46 chromosomes. The nucleus of a cell copies the chromosomes to **double** that number during **interphase**. The cell then moves a copy to each end of the cell during **mitosis**. The cell then divides during **cytokinesis**, making two new cells each with 46 chromosomes.

2 Complete the numbers inside the cells to show what happens to the number of chromosomes during mitosis.

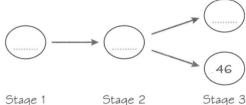

Stage 1   Stage 2   Stage 3

3 a Describe what is happening inside the cell between stages 1 and 2.

....

....

b Describe what is happening inside the cell between stages 2 and 3.

....

....

Meiosis is a different type of cell division where four cells are made from one cell. In females, meiosis takes place in the ovaries, where it produces eggs. In males, meiosis takes place in the testes, where it produces sperm. The four cells that are made from the original parent cell each have a different half set of chromosomes.

4 Complete the numbers inside the cells to show what happens to the number of chromosomes during meiosis.

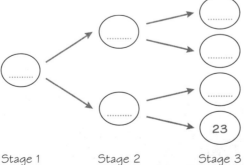

Stage 1   Stage 2   Stage 3

First meiosis makes two cells, each with a full set of chromosomes.

These divide again to make four cells, each with a half set of chromosomes.

1 How can I identify the stages in the cell cycle?

The first stage of the cell cycle is **interphase**, where the cell makes new components and a copy of each chromosome.

Then, during **mitosis**, four stages happen: **prophase**, **metaphase**, **anaphase** and **telophase**. The chromosomes move apart and the nucleus divides.

The cell cycle ends with **cytokinesis** (cell division). The two new cells that are produced are genetically identical and are called **daughter cells**.

① The diagram below shows the stages of mitosis and the splitting of the cell.

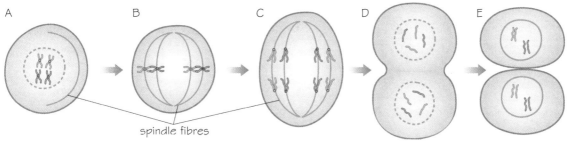

spindle fibres

a Name the stages of mitosis A, B, C and D.

A .... C ....

B .... D ....

b What process is happening in E? ....

> This is where the cell divides into two new identical cells.

c Describe what is happening in stages B and C.

....

> What needs to happen before the nucleus divides?

....

② The cell cycle in a tomato plant tip cell lasts 6 hours.

a Convert 6 hours to minutes.

....

b Work out the number of minutes represented by a 1° angle on the pie chart.

....

Interphase

320°

20° Mitosis

20° Cytokinesis

c Use the information in the pie chart to complete the table and calculate the time taken for each stage of the cell cycle.

> How many cells will there be after 6 h?

	Angle (°)	Time in minutes	Time in hours and minutes
Interphase			
Mitosis			
Cytokinesis			

③ Tomato plants have 10 chromosomes in a normal cell.

a How many chromosomes are there in a cell 5 h 20 min after the start of the cell cycle? ....

> Look at where the cell cycle will be after 5 h 20 min.

b How many chromosomes are there in a cell 6 h after the start of the cell cycle? ....

Biology

② How can I describe situations where mitosis is occurring?

Mitosis is used for increasing the number of cells during growth, when replacing damaged cells and for asexual reproduction. Mitosis produces genetically identical cells. This means that all cells in the body have exactly the same set of chromosomes.

Asexual reproduction leads to offspring produced from only one parent. All the offspring are identical and are known as clones.

Genes are sections of DNA found on chromosomes. Humans have 46 chromosomes in the nucleus of normal body cells. The nucleus controls the chemical reactions inside the cell.

① Look at the diagram and number ✎ the parts of the cell in order of size with 1 as the smallest and 3 as the largest.

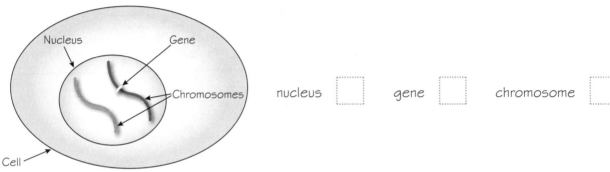

nucleus ☐   gene ☐   chromosome ☐

② Human skin cells A, B, C and D in the diagram have just been produced to replace some damaged cells.

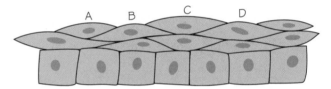

a Name ✎ the type of cell division that has produced these new cells.

....

b What happens to the genetic material before the cell divides? ✎

....

c How many chromosomes will be in cell A? ✎

....

d Why is it important that skin cells can divide? ✎

....

③ The diagram shows a nucleus just before the nucleus begins to divide during mitosis. Complete ✎ the second diagram to show what the nucleus of a cell produced by this mitosis looks like.

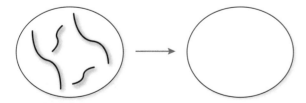

You could use this to help you remember what mitosis does.

Makes	Makes
I	Identical
Toes	T
O	Offspring
Skin	S
I	I
S	S

Remember Mitosis produces identical cells. This means that the cells will have an identical number of chromosomes.

3 How can I explain the importance of meiosis?

Meiosis is the type of cell division that makes sperm cells and eggs. Meiosis involves two divisions. First, two cells are made with full sets of chromosomes. These two cells then divide to make four **non-identical** cells which can be used in sexual reproduction. Each **gamete** contains half of the chromosomes needed to make a full set. They join together during fertilisation to form a **zygote.**

Gamete A sex cell such as egg or sperm. Gametes are formed by meiosis.

(1) Which diagram represents cell division by meiosis? Circle (A) one letter.

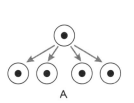

A

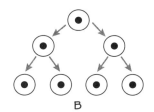

B

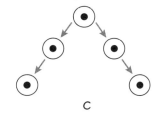

C

You could use this to help you remember what meiosis does.

Makes
Eggs
I
O
Sperm
I
S

(2) Name ✏ an organ where meiosis takes place.

....

Alleles are different versions of the same gene. For example, one chromosome could carry the allele for blue eyes and the other chromosome could carry the allele for brown eyes.

(3) In this diagram the top cell contains two alleles for two different genes.
B is the gene for brown eyes and b the gene for blue eyes.
F is the gene for brown hair and f is the gene for blond hair.

Write ✏ the letters in the boxes to make four different combinations of alleles from these two genes, just like during meiosis.

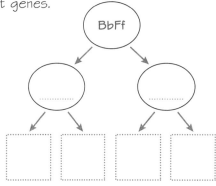

The **diploid** number in human cells is **46** chromosomes. The **haploid** number is **23**. Most body cells contain 46 chromosomes, but eggs or sperm cells only contain 23 chromosomes.

Diploid comes from the Greek for 'double' and **haploid** means 'half'.

(4) Circle (A) the correct keywords in this passage.

Meiosis **doubles** / **halves** / **triples** the number of chromosomes and leads to **identical** / **non-identical** / **cloned** cells.

In meiosis the cell divides twice. The first division produces two cells with the same number of chromosomes as in the original full set in the parent cell (called the **triploid** / **diploid** / **haploid** number). The second division divides those two cells and reduces the number of chromosomes to half the number in the original parent cell. The four cells now have the **triploid** / **diploid** / **haploid** number of chromosomes. This reduction is essential for **sexual** / **asexual** reproduction and **increases** / **maintains** / **decreases** genetic variety.

Biology

Sample response

Your understanding of mitosis, meiosis and the cell cycle will often be tested in the context of living things. Read this question carefully, use your knowledge and consider your response.

Look at this exam-style question and the answers given by a student.

Exam-style question

1   **(a)**   Mitosis and meiosis are types of cell division. Complete the table below to show whether mitosis or meiosis is being described. Place **one** tick in each row.

Example of cell division	Mitosis	Meiosis
Gametes made in the testes	✓	✓
Growth of an embryo		
A yeast cell budding to produce offspring	✓	
Non identical cells are produced		✓

(4 marks)

   (b)   The diagram shows a cell dividing.

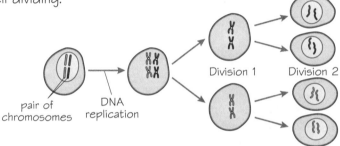

pair of chromosomes   DNA replication   Division 1   Division 2

Identify the type of cell division shown. Give three reasons for your decision.

Meiosis because the cell divides twice to produce four cells.

(3 marks)

   (c)   Growth involves mitosis. Explain why growth does not involve meiosis.

Meiosis produces cells that are not identical. The cells produced do not have

the same genes and therefore they are not the same. The original cell has

46 chromosomes but the cells produced by meiosis have only 23 chromosomes,

and the chromosomes are all different.

(3 marks)

① Give ✏ **two** reasons why this student did not get all four marks for **(a)**.

....

....

② How could the student have achieved more marks for **(b)**? ✏

....

....

③ The student scored 2 marks for **(c)**. What extra response could have achieved the third mark for **(c)**? ✏

....

Your turn!

Now use what you have learned to answer this question.

Remember to read the question thoroughly, looking for clues.

Make good use of your knowledge. Read each feature carefully, use the additional guidance below and apply your knowledge from other areas of biology.

Exam-style question

1 Mitosis and meiosis are types of cell division.

(a) Complete the table to show which of the features are produced by mitosis and which are produced by meiosis.

Feature	Mitosis or meiosis?
Production of egg cells	
A lizard growing a new tail	
Production of pollen in a flower	
Cells replaced on the skin to heal a cut	

(4 marks)

- Eggs need to contain only half the genetic information; this is the haploid number.
- Some animals can grow new body parts identical to the original one.
- Pollen in plants is similar to sperm in animals.
- Lots of new cells are made on both sides of a cut until they meet in the middle.

(b) Name the organs that produce gametes (sex cells) in a man and in a woman.

Think about which organs make sperm and eggs.

A man ....

A woman .... (2 marks)

(c) Describe two differences between mitosis and meiosis.

What type of cells are made? Where are they made? How many are made? What are the cells used for?

....

....

....

....

.... (2 marks)

Need more practice?

You need to be able to recognise where mitosis and meiosis are occurring in a given situation. Often, you will be tested on your understanding of both types of cell division in the same question.

Have a go at this exam-style question.

Exam-style question

1   The diagram shows two types of cell division.

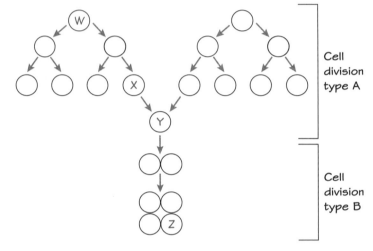

(a)   Name the type of cell division labelled as type A.

....   (1 mark)

(b)   Name the type of cell division labelled as type B.

....   (1 mark)

(c)   Identify cell Y.

....   (1 mark)

Cell W contains 8 picograms of DNA. (1 picogram = 10^{-12} grams)

(d)   Calculate the mass in picograms of DNA in cell X.

....   (1 mark)

Boost your grade

To improve your grade, make sure you can:
- understand the stages of the cell cycle and of mitosis
- recognise and describe mitosis occurring in different situations
- explain that meiosis halves the number of chromosomes but fertilisation restores a full set.

How confident do you feel about each of these **skills?** Colour in 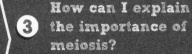 the bars.

1   How can I identify the stages in the cell cycle?

2   How can I describe situations where mitosis is occurring?

3   How can I explain the importance of meiosis?

④ Practical skills

This unit will help you to answer questions based on practical work and practical situations.

In the exam, you will be expected to answer questions such as the one below.

Exam-style question

1 A student investigated how reaction time is affected by the time of day. This is the method:

1 The subject should be seated.

2 A ruler is held between the thumb and forefinger.

3 When the ruler is dropped the subject must catch it as quickly as possible.

4 The reaction time is measured by how far the ruler dropped before being caught.

5 This test was repeated at different times of day.

(a) Name the dependent variable in this investigation.

.... (1 mark)

(b) State **two** variables that need to be kept constant during the investigation.

.... (2 marks)

The student's results are shown in **Table 1**.

Table 1

Name	Time of day	Distance ruler fell (cm)
Peter	8.30 am	12.6
Georgina	8.30 am	14.2
Anya	3.30 pm	11.5
David	3.30 pm	16.1

(c) Explain why the results in **Table 1** do not allow a valid comparison.

.... (2 marks)

You will already have done some work on practical skills. Before starting the **skills boosts**, rate your confidence in each area. Colour in 🖉 the bars.

① How do I identify the independent, dependent and control variables?

② How do I ensure my method has sufficient detail?

③ How do I draw a results table?

Many factors, known as variables, may affect the results of an experiment. When writing a method you must describe clearly how all these variables will be altered, measured or kept constant.

A **variable** is any factor that can change or be changed in the experiment.

- The **independent variable** is the factor you change.

- The **dependent variable** is what you measure for your results.

The dependent variable is affected by changes in the independent variable.

- A **control variable** is any factor that could affect the results of the experiment and which must be kept constant.

Read the following extract from an experimental procedure.

1 Pour 2 cm³ of 1% catalase enzyme solution into a test tube.

2 Pour 5 cm³ of 2% hydrogen peroxide into another test tube.

3 Place both tubes in a water bath at 25 °C.

4 After 2 minutes, pour the catalase into the hydrogen peroxide.

5 Measure the height of the bubbles given off in 10 seconds.

6 Repeat at 35 °C, 45 °C, 55 °C and 75 °C.

① ⓐ Underline Ⓐ the independent variable and highlight ✎ the dependent variable in the box below.

> catalase concentration   hydrogen peroxide concentration
>
> temperature   time   height of bubbles

The independent variable is changed and the dependent variable is measured.

ⓑ How is the independent variable altered? ✎

....

ⓒ How is the volume of enzyme solution kept constant? ✎

....

ⓓ How is the concentration of hydrogen peroxide kept constant? ✎

....

All your results should be put together in one results table.

- The independent variable should be in the left-hand column.

- The dependent variable should be in the right-hand column.

- Your column headings should also have the units.

② Here is a results table for this experiment. Add ✎ the column headings.

The volume of enzyme solution and the concentration of hydrogen peroxide are **control variables**. Can you think of any other variables that should be kept constant in this experiment?

25	10
35	20
45	55
55	50
75	0

How do I identify the independent, dependent and control variables?

Variables are any factors that can change or be changed in the experiment. There will be one independent variable, one dependent variable and many other variables (the control variables) that should be kept constant.

The **independent variable** is the variable or factor you change. It is unaffected by other variables.

1. Circle Ⓐ the independent variable in the following experiments.

   a. An investigation into the effect of substrate concentration on the activity of amylase.

   b. An investigation into the effect of pH on the breakdown of protein.

> The independent variable is the effect you are investigating. It is the variable you deliberately decide to change during the experiment.

The **dependent variable** is the factor that changes as a result of changing the independent variable. It is dependent upon the independent variable.

2. Underline Ⓐ the dependent variable in the following experiments.

   a. Investigating the action of pectinase on the clarity of apple juice.

   b. The effect of salt concentration on the length of a potato chip.

> The dependent variable is what you measure and gives you your results in the experiment.

A **control variable** must be kept constant. Control variables will be all the other variables except the independent and dependent variables. Control variables may include pH, temperature, light intensity, volume of enzyme, volume of substrate, carbon dioxide concentration, and so on.

> Control variables are factors that may affect the results. There will be many variables you need to keep constant. In an exam question do not repeat control variables that have already been described.

3. In each experiment, write ✏ **two** variables that should be kept constant.

   a. Investigating how light intensity affects the rate of photosynthesis.

   ....

   b. Investigating how pH affects the activity of the enzyme amylase.

   ....

4. A student used the apparatus shown in the diagram to investigate the rate of water loss from a leafy twig. The student altered the speed of the air movement.

   a. What is the independent variable? ✏ ....

   b. What is the dependent variable? ✏ ....

   c. Write ✏ three variables that must be controlled to improve the results.

   ....

   ....

   ....

rubber tubing
capillary tube
bubble in water
water

2 How do I ensure my method has sufficient detail?

The method for an experiment must be detailed. It should describe:
- how the independent variable is altered
- how the dependent variable is measured
- how the control variables are kept constant.

This apparatus was used to investigate the effect of light intensity on the rate of photosynthesis in pondweed.

The method for an experiment should be detailed enough for another student to repeat the same experiment in exactly the same way.

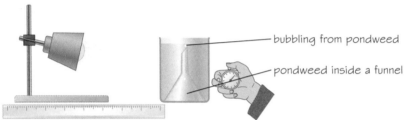

bubbling from pondweed

pondweed inside a funnel

1 Light intensity is the independent variable. How is the light intensity altered? Tick ✓ the correct answer.

What is the purpose of the ruler?

moving the light ☐ using a different light ☐

using two lights ☐ removing the light shade ☐

2 The rate of photosynthesis is the dependent variable. How is the rate of photosynthesis measured? Circle Ⓐ the correct answer.

What is being counted?

> counting the number of bubbles released per minute
>
> recording the volume of each bubble
>
> measuring the time between each bubble
>
> measuring the depth of water in the beaker

3 A student listed the variables that must be kept constant. In each case describe 🖉 how the variable could be kept constant.

Adding a little sodium hydrogen carbonate to the water will release CO_2.

a Time for counting of bubbles ....

....

b Concentration of CO_2 ....

....

4 Complete 🖉 the sentences to describe the method.

Note that the steps in a method are often lettered or given numbers rather than written as continuous text.

1 Set up the apparatus as shown in the diagram.

2 Place a lamp at 5 cm from the .... and cover with a glass funnel.

3 Leave the pondweed for .... minutes to start photosynthesising constantly.

4 Count the number of bubbles given off each ....

5 Repeat steps .... and .... with the lamp at distances of 10, ..., ... and 40 cm.

3   How do I draw a results table?

All the results from a practical should be recorded in one results table. The format of the table is very important.
- The **independent variable** always goes in the **left-hand column** of a results table (or on the top row).
- The **dependent variable** always goes in the **right-hand column** of a results table (or on the lower row).
- The **units** should always go in the column headings, not in the main part of the table.

① A student carried out an investigation to test the effect of temperature on the time taken to digest protein. She carried out three trials and calculated a mean.

Complete 🖉 the column headings in the table. Remember to include the units.

What is the usual unit of temperature?

What is the usual unit of time?

		Trial 1	Trial 2	Trial 3	mean
	20				
	40				

② A student prepared the following results table for an experiment in which he tested the effect of light intensity on the rate of photosynthesis.

Rate of photosynthesis				Light intensity
Trial 1	Trial 2	Trial 3	mean	

You need to work out which is the independent variable and which is the dependent variable.

a Circle Ⓐ the independent variable.

b Give 🖉 **two** things that are wrong with this table of results.

Which variable should be in the first column?

....

....

③ A student carried out an investigation to determine the effect of changing the temperature on the rate of water loss from a leafy shoot. The loss of water was measured by weighing the plant. The student carried out three trials at 10 °C, 20 °C and 30 °C, and calculated a mean for each temperature.

a Circle Ⓐ the independent variable.

b Underline Ⓐ the dependent variable.

c Draw 🖉 a results table for this investigation.

Biology

Sample response

Your practical skills will usually be tested in the context of a real practical that has been described. Read the question carefully, use your knowledge and consider your response.

Look at this exam-style question and the answers given by a student.

Exam-style question

1 A student investigated the effect of concentration on the rate of diffusion.

This was the method:

1 Take five Petri dishes containing colourless agar gel.

2 Use a cork borer to make a small well (hole) in the centre of the agar.

3 Pour each dilution of food dye into a well and leave for 20 minutes.

4 Measure the spread of food dye.

(a) (i) State the independent variable in the student's experiment.

concentration

(1 mark)

(ii) Give an additional detail the student should have included in the method.

the range of concentrations used

(1 mark)

After 20 minutes, the agar dishes looked like this:

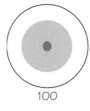

100   80   60   40   10

(b) Complete the results table.

Concentration as % of original	100	80	60	40	10
Spread of dye	22	17	15	12	6

(4 marks)

(c) Explain why the result for 60% food dye is difficult to measure.

The dye was not evenly spread.

(1 mark)

(d) State **two** factors that should have been kept constant in this experiment.

time, temperature, thickness of agar plate, colour of dye

(2 marks)

(1) How could the student have improved their answer to (a)?   Concentration of what?

....

(2) What important detail has the student missed in their answer to (b)?

....

(3) How many variables was the student asked to give in (d)?   Read the question carefully so that you don't waste time!

....

Your turn!

It is now time to use what you have learned to answer this exam-style question.

Remember to read the question thoroughly, looking for clues.

Make good use of your knowledge from other areas of biology.

Exam-style question

1   A student investigated how reaction time is affected by the time of day. This is the method:

   1   The subject should be seated.

   2   A ruler is held between the thumb and forefinger.

   3   When the ruler is dropped the subject must catch it as quickly as possible.

   4   The reaction time is measured by how far the ruler dropped before being caught.

   5   This test was repeated at different times of day.

   (a)   Name the dependent variable in this investigation.

   This is the thing you measure during the practical.

   ....   **(1 mark)**

   (b)   State **two** variables that need to be kept constant during the investigation.

   Think about things that might affect the reaction time and how far the ruler falls.

   ....

   ....   **(2 marks)**

The student's results are shown in **Table 1**.

Table 1

Name	Time of day	Distance ruler fell (cm)
Peter	8.30 am	12.6
Georgina	8.30 am	14.2
Anya	3.30 pm	11.5
David	3.30 pm	16.1

   (c)   Explain why the results in **Table 1** do not allow a valid comparison.

   Think about whether all the possible variables were kept the same for each test.

   ....

   ....

   ....

   ....   **(2 marks)**

Need more practice?

In the exam, questions about practical skills could ask you to:
- write a method
- suggest improvements to a method
- complete a results table.

Have a go at this exam-style question.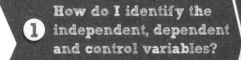

Exam-style question

1 A student investigated the distribution of daisy plants around a large tree.

She decided to investigate whether shade created by the tree affects how many daisies grow. She placed a quadrat in the shade and counted how many daisy plants were in the quadrat. She repeated the process in the sunlight further from the tree. Her results are recorded in the table.

| | Number of daisies in quadrat | | | |
	Quadrat 1	Quadrat 2	Quadrat 3	mean
In shade	3	1	4	
In sun	6	4	7	

(a) Calculate the mean number of daisies per quadrat in the shade, and the mean number per quadrat in the sun. Write these values, to one decimal place, in the table.

(2 marks)

(b) Give an additional detail that the student could have included in her method.

....

....

....

....

(3 marks)

How confident do you feel about each of these **skills?** Colour in 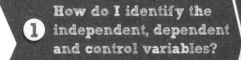 the bars.

1 How do I identify the independent, dependent and control variables?

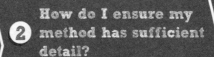
2 How do I ensure my method has sufficient detail?

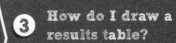
3 How do I draw a results table?

⑤ Interpreting graphs

This unit will help you to understand how to make full use of data when the data is presented in the form of a graph.

In the exam, you will be asked to tackle questions such as the one below.

1   A student measured the length of the root of a bean seedling as it germinated and grew over a number of days. The results are shown in the graph.

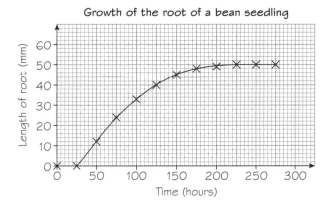

Growth of the root of a bean seedling

(a)   Describe the growth of the root over the first 100 hours.

.... (3 marks)

(b)   State the maximum length of the root.

.... (1 mark)

(c)   Explain why the root did not appear to grow for the first 25 hours.

.... (2 marks)

You will already have done some work on graphs. Before starting the **skills boosts**, rate your confidence in each area. Colour in 🖉 the bars.

1   **How do I read data accurately from a graph?**

2   **How do I describe what a graph shows?**

3   **How do I explain the shape of a graph?**

Biology

You may be asked to describe or explain the trend shown by a graph, read data from a graph or describe the shape of a graph. You must read all the information on the graph carefully.

Use this graph for all the questions on this page.

Variation in percentage cover of reeds with distance from pond

① To describe a graph, first make sure you understand the graph.

a What does this graph show? 🖊

Use the axis labels, including the units, in your answer.

....

....

....

....

....

b Describe the trend shown by the graph. Tick ✓ the sentence that gives the best description.

When asked to **describe the trend**, you need to say what happens as the value of the **independent variable** increases.

A   As distance from the pond increases, the % cover of reeds increases. ☐

B   As distance from the pond increases, the % cover of reeds decreases. ☐

C   As the % cover of reeds increases, the distance from the pond increases. ☐

D   As the % cover of reeds increases, the distance from the pond decreases. ☐

② **a** What is the percentage cover of reeds 4 metres from the pond? Circle Ⓐ the correct answer.

| 9%   10%   13%   15%   20% |

Work out what one square represents on each axis (the two axes have different scales). Then find 4 metres on the horizontal axis. Draw a vertical line up to the graph line, then draw a horizontal line across to the vertical axis.

b How far from the pond do you need to go before you stop finding reeds? Underline Ⓐ the correct distance.

| 2 m   5 m   6 m   7 m   8 m |

This question is asking you to give the distance where the percentage cover first reaches zero.

③ Explain 🖊 what the data in the graph tells you about the conditions the reeds prefer.

....

....

....

....

....

....

First you need to use the data to **describe** where the reeds grow – your answer to ① will help. Then use your biology knowledge to **explain** why the reeds grow where they do. Write a conclusion about the conditions reed plants prefer.

1 How do I read data accurately from a graph?

You may be asked to read data values from a graph. When you describe a graph, you need to include data values in your description, even if the question does not specifically ask you to.

Before you answer any questions about a graph, read the title and the axis labels, including the units. Then think about what the graph is showing you.

This graph shows the results of an investigation. The rate of reaction is measured in cubic centimetres of oxygen gas released per second (cm^3/s).

Effect of substrate concentration on rate of reaction

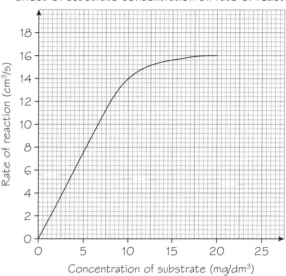

1 a What is the maximum rate of the reaction?

.... cm^3/s

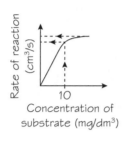

The 'maximum' is the highest value. Draw a line from the highest point of the graph to the 'rate of reaction' axis.

b What is the rate of reaction at a substrate

concentration of 10 mg/dm^3? .... cm^3/s

Find 10 mg/dm^3 on the 'concentration of substrate' axis. Draw a line up to the graph line, and then across to the 'rate of reaction' axis.

c What concentration of substrate produces a rate

of reaction of 6 cm^3/s? .... mg/dm^3

2 a For what values of concentration of substrate is the graph a straight line? ....

b What shape is the graph for concentrations above 8 mg/dm^3?

....

c Complete these sentences to describe the shape of the graph. Use data values.

Give the data values where the shape of the graph changes.

As the .... of substrate increases from 0 to 8 mg/dm^3

the rate of reaction .... from 0 to .... cm^3/s.

This section of the graph is a .... line, which shows the

rate of reaction is increasing at a .... rate.

For concentrations of substrate greater than 8 mg/dm^3 the graph is

a .... line. The rate of reaction levels off to reach a

maximum of .... cm^3/s at a substrate concentration of

.... mg/dm^3.

You need to use your maths knowledge here. What does a straight line with a positive gradient tell you?

Biology

2 How do I describe what a graph shows?

A good description of a graph:
- describes how the dependent variable changes as the independent variable increases
- describes the shape of the graph and includes data values
- explains what the shape of the graph shows in context.

A graph shows how the dependent variable changes as the independent variable is changed.

1) Look at the title and axis labels on this graph.

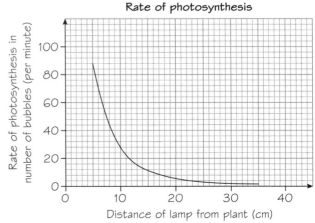

Rate of photosynthesis

a What is the independent variable? 🖉

The independent variable is always on the horizontal axis.

....

b What is the dependent variable? 🖉

Include the units with the variables.

....

c Circle Ⓐ the correct word in the sentence below.

As the independent variable increases, the dependent variable **increases** / **decreases**.

d Complete 🖉 the sentence below to describe what the graph shows.

As the distance of the lamp from the plant increases, the rate of

photosynthesis ....

'As the {independent variable} increases, the {dependent variable} …

e Complete 🖉 the sentence below to describe the shape of the graph. Circle Ⓐ the correct word from the choice of bold words.

The graph is a .... It **falls** / **rises** steeply for

distances from 6 cm to .... and then falls

more / **less** steeply, reaching zero at a distance of

.... cm from the lamp.

Is the graph a curve or a straight line? Where is it steep? Where does the steepness change?

f Complete 🖉 this sentence to explain what the shape of the graph shows. Circle Ⓐ the correct word from the choice of bold words.

The rate of photosynthesis decreases **quickly** / **slowly** for

distances from .... cm to 10 cm, and then

decreases more **quickly** / **slowly** until it reaches zero at a

distance of .... cm from the lamp.

f asks you to explain the changes in shape you described in e, in the context of the plant.

3 How do I explain the shape of a graph?

You need to use your biological knowledge to give reasons why a graph has the shape it has. There may be clues in the question to help you.

Exam-style question

1 Plants use light as a source of energy.

A student wanted to investigate the effect of light intensity on the rate of photosynthesis.

The student placed a piece of pondweed in a beaker of water and used a table lamp to provide light.

The results are shown in the graph.

Explain the shape of the curve.

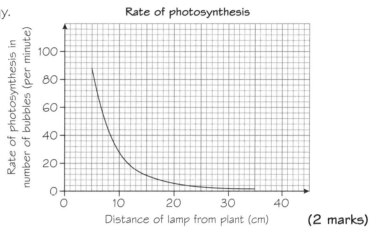

(2 marks)

① What was the student investigating?

....

....

② How did the student vary the light intensity? Tick ✓ the box showing the correct answer.

A By moving the lamp away from the beaker of pondweed.

B By varying the brightness of the lamp.

C By increasing the number of lamps.

D By conducting the experiment in bright sunlight and then at night.

It is always the independent variable that is varied in an experiment.

③ Explain why plants need light for photosynthesis.

....

....

④ Complete the paragraph below to describe the shape of the curve and explain what the experiment shows.

Plants need light for .... The light is a source of ....

The higher the light .... the more energy there is for photosynthesis.

As the distance from the lamp increases, the light intensity .... and

the rate of photosynthesis .... quickly. At distances over 10 cm from

the lamp the rate of .... decreases more slowly, until it reaches

zero at a distance of .... from the lamp.

Use your description of this graph from page 36 to help you.

Biology

Sample response

You may be expected to make use of graphs as part of a question about practical work or be asked to interpret data from a survey.

Look at this exam-style question and the answers given by a student.

Exam-style question

1 The graph shows the percentage of people dying from coronary heart disease (CHD) for smokers and non-smokers.

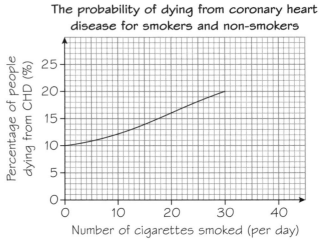

The probability of dying from coronary heart disease for smokers and non-smokers

(a) A man smokes 30 cigarettes a day. State the probability that he will die from CHD.

   20
_____ (1 mark)

(b) The man reduces the number of cigarettes he smokes each day from 30 to 15. State how this affects the probability that he will die from CHD.

   The probability of dying from CHD decreases. It halves from 20 to 10.
_____ (2 marks)

(c) Describe the shape of the graph and explain what it shows.

   The graph is a curve, which rises steadily. The graph shows that smoking causes

   cancer, as the more cigarettes smoked per day the more likely you are to get

   cancer. Someone who does not smoke has a 10% chance of dying but this rises to

   20% if they smoke 30 cigarettes a day
_____ (3 marks)

① In (a) the student has given the correct number. What is missing? ✎ ....

② In (b) the student is incorrect in saying the chances of dying are halved.
Write ✎ the correct answer.

....

③ How many marks would you give the student's response to (c)? Highlight ✎ the parts of the answer you would give a mark. Then explain ✎ why you gave this number of marks.

....

....

....

Your turn!

It is now time to use what you have learned to answer this exam-style question.
Remember to read the question thoroughly, looking for clues.
Read the graph title and labels, and write a clear description.
Make good use of your biological knowledge.

Read the exam-style question and answer ✏ it using the hints below.

Exam-style question

1   A student measured the length of the root of a bean seedling as it germinated and grew over a number of days. The results are shown in the graph.

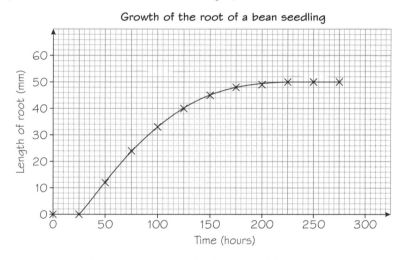

Growth of the root of a bean seedling

(a)   Describe the growth of the root over the first 100 hours.

Describe the shape of the graph and say what this means. Give data values.

....

....

....

....   (3 marks)

(b)   State the maximum length of the root. ....

....   (1 mark)

Draw lines from the graph line to the axes to help you read the value accurately.

(c)   Explain why the root did not appear to grow for the first 25 hours.

....

....

....   (2 marks)

What must happen before a seed can begin to grow? What does the seed need to absorb from the surroundings?

Need more practice?

When a question includes a graph, first read the graph title and axis labels, look at the overall shape of the graph, and work out what it is showing you. Then you are ready to answer the questions.

1 The graph shows the relative risk of an accident while driving, plotted against the blood alcohol level.

(a) Describe how the risk of having an accident changes as the blood alcohol level increases.

> Start your answer with 'As the blood alcohol level increases, ...'
>
> Note that the command word is '**describe**'. You are not asked to *explain* why blood alcohol levels make someone a more dangerous driver.

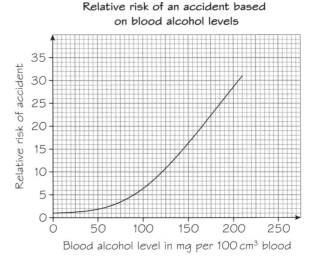

Relative risk of an accident based on blood alcohol levels

....

....

.... (3 marks)

(b) The legal limit for driving is a blood alcohol level of 80 mg per 100 cm³ of blood. Give the relative risk of having an accident at this blood alcohol level.

Draw lines on the graph to help you.

.... (1 mark)

(c) The relative risk of having an accident with no alcohol in the blood is set at 1. Give the blood alcohol level when the risk is 10 times greater.

.... (1 mark)

Be ready to answer questions about graphs in any question about practical work. You may also see graphs linked to questions about health. These questions may link diseases to aspects of lifestyle such as diet, obesity, smoking and alcohol consumption. In each case you may be asked to explain why the lifestyle has an effect on health.

How confident do you feel about each of these **skills?** Colour in the bars.

1 How do I read data accurately from a graph?

2 How do I describe what a graph shows?

3 How do I explain the shape of a graph?

⑥ Maths skills

This unit will help you to understand how to carry out simple calculations, such as working out the magnification of a diagram or the rate of a reaction, and calculating percentages.

In the exam, you will be asked to tackle questions such as the one below.

Exam-style question

1   The graph shows the growth of a root plotted against time.

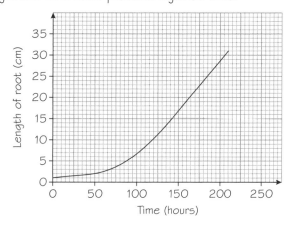

(a)   Give the length of the root at 120 hours.

....   (1 mark)

(b)   Calculate the rate of growth of the root between 120 and 150 hours.
       Show your working.

....   (2 marks)

(c)   Calculate the percentage increase in root length between 120 and 180 hours.
       Show your working.

....   (3 marks)

You will already have done some work on this topic. Before starting the **skills boosts**, rate your confidence in the maths skills needed in biology. Colour in 🖉 the bars.

1 How do I calculate magnification?

2 How do I calculate the rate of a reaction?

3 How do I calculate a percentage?

Magnification is how many times bigger the image is than the object you are viewing.

$$\text{magnification} = \frac{\text{size of image}}{\text{size of object}}$$

(1) Calculate the magnification of this image by following steps
a, **b** and **c** below.

object

image

a First, write ✎ the length of the object and the length of the image in the same units.

length of object = 6 mm

length of image = ... mm

b Now substitute ✎ those values into the equation.

$$\text{magnification} = \frac{\text{size of image}}{\text{size of object}} = \frac{}{}$$

You might be asked to do this calculation for the **length** or the **width** of an object.

c Write ✎ the answer.

magnification = × ....

Remember Insert a multiplication sign, ×, before the value to show it is the magnification. Magnification does not have units.

The **rate of a reaction** is the amount of product produced in one unit of time. To calculate the rate of reaction, divide the amount of product produced by the time taken.

(2) In a reaction, 20 cm^3 of oxygen is released in 5 seconds. Calculate the rate of the reaction by following steps **a**, **b** and **c** below.

a First, write ✎ the amount produced and the time taken.

.... cm^3 produced in .... seconds.

b Divide ✎ both sides by the same amount to work out the amount of product produced in 1 second.

÷ 5 ⟶ 20 cm^3 in 5 s ⟵ ÷ 5

.... cm^3 in .... s

c Give ✎ the rate of reaction.

rate of reaction = ... cm^3/s

To write one number as a percentage of another, first write the two numbers as a fraction, then convert to a decimal and then convert to a percentage.

(3) In a survey of a field, 4 out of 15 quadrats contain daisy plants. Calculate the percentage of the quadrats that contain daisy plants by following steps **a**, **b** and **c**.

a Complete ✎ the fraction: $\dfrac{4}{}$

b Convert the fraction to a decimal by dividing. Use a calculator. Complete ✎ the fraction and decimal.

$$\frac{4}{} = \text{.................................}$$

c Convert ✎ the decimal to a percentage by multiplying by 100. Round your answer to 1 d.p.

How do I calculate magnification?

> Remember that magnification is how many times larger the image is compared to the object.
>
> The formula for magnification is: $\text{magnification} = \dfrac{\text{size of image}}{\text{size of object}}$
>
> Always use the same units for both measurements.
>
> You can compare:
>
> - the length of the object and the length of the image or
> - the width of the object and the width of the image.

(1) A guard cell is 0.04 mm in length. A student draws a diagram of a guard cell that is 80 mm in length. Calculate the magnification of the student's diagram by following steps (a), (b) and (c) below.

   (a) Write ✏ the length of the object and the image in the same units.

     length of object = ...   length of image = ...

   (b) Substitute ✏ those values into the equation:

$$\text{magnification} = \frac{\text{size of image}}{\text{size of object}} = \frac{\boxed{}}{\boxed{}} = \text{.....................}$$

   (c) Write ✏ your final answer.

     magnification = × ....

> **Remember** Always insert a multiplication sign before the value to show it is the magnification and remember that magnification does not have units.

You may be told the magnification and image size, and asked to calculate the actual size of an object. Magnification is how many times larger the image is compared to the object.

If the magnification is ×200:

- the image is 200 times larger than the object   object → ×200 → image
- the object is 200 times smaller than the image   image → ÷200 → object

(2) The image of a cell is 5 mm across. The magnification is ×200. Calculate the actual size of the cell by following steps (a), (b) and (c) below.

   (a) Write ✏ the equation to calculate the actual size.

Use this triangle to help you rearrange the magnification equation.

$M = \dfrac{I}{A}$

$A = \dfrac{I}{M}$

$I = A \times M$

   (b) Substitute ✏ in the values from the question.

   (c) Write ✏ the actual size of the cell. Remember to include the units. ....

Biology

2 How do I calculate the rate of a reaction?

A **rate** tells you how much a quantity changes in one unit of time. The unit of time can be seconds, hours, days, years, etc.

1 Calculate the rate of photosynthesis when $24\,cm^3$ of oxygen gas is released in 3 minutes.

a First, write 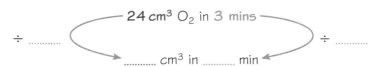 the amount of oxygen produced and the time.

.... cm^3 produced in .... minutes

b Divide both sides by the same amount to work out the amount produced in 1 unit of time.

$÷$ .... — $24\,cm^3\ O_2$ in 3 mins — $÷$ ....

.... cm^3 in .... min

c Give the rate of reaction.

rate of reaction = ... cm^3/minute

The quantity of oxygen is measured in cm^3 and the time is measured in minutes, so the rate is in cm^3/min.

Sometimes you may be asked to calculate the rate using information from a results table.

2 A student investigated diffusion of food colouring in agar gel. The table shows the distance diffused from the centre of the gel over a period of time.

Time (hours)	0	1	2	3	4
Distance colouring diffused from centre (mm)	0	8	14	24	30

a What was the rate of diffusion in the first hour? ....

b What was the rate of diffusion in the final hour? ....

You may also be asked to calculate a rate from a graph.

3 The graph shows the length of a root plotted against time.

Work through the stages below to find out the rate of growth between 25 hours and 75 hours.

a Write the increase in length and the time taken.

.... mm growth in .... hours

b Divide the increase in length by the number of hours. Complete the calculation.

rate of growth = $\dfrac{\boxed{}\ mm}{\boxed{}\ hours}$

c Write the answer for the rate of growth.

rate of growth = ... mm/hour

③ How do I calculate a percentage?

'Per cent' means 'out of 100'. You may be asked to calculate a simple percentage or a percentage change.

Follow these steps to work out a percentage:

1 Write the two numbers as a fraction: $\dfrac{\text{quantity you are interested in}}{\text{total quantity}}$

2 Convert the fraction to a decimal by division, then multiply by 100.

> Round the final percentage value to 1 decimal place, unless the question tells you to round differently.

① In a reaction, 80 mg of starch reduces to 24 mg. Calculate ✐ the percentage of starch that is left.

> Write the fraction:
> $\dfrac{\text{amount of starch at end}}{\text{amount of starch at beginning}}$

Tick ✓ the correct answer.

24.0% ☐   30.0% ☐   56.0% ☐   80.0% ☐

② In a survey of 45 692 people with type 2 diabetes, 29 435 people are overweight.

Calculate ✐ the percentage of people who are overweight.

Tick ✓ the correct answer.

35.6% ☐   45.6% ☐   64% ☐   64.4% ☐

To calculate a percentage change (increase or decrease), calculate the actual change first.

Then use this equation: $\dfrac{\text{actual change}}{\text{original value}} \times 100$

③ Calculate the percentage change when a population rises from 345 000 to 385 000.

ⓐ Calculate ✐ the actual change by subtraction. ....

ⓑ Write ✐ the original value. ....

ⓒ Substitute ✐ the two values into the equation to calculate the percentage change. Use a calculator.

> A positive percentage change is a percentage increase, a negative percentage change is a percentage decrease.

④ A farmer uses a new fertiliser. His crop increases from 324 tonnes to 352 tonnes. Calculate ✐ the percentage increase in the farmer's crop.

Biology

Sample response

You may have to carry out several calculations in your exam. Calculations can be part of a theory question, or a practical question or a question on health and disease.

Look at these exam-style questions and the answers given by a student.

1 The photo shows the bacterium *Vibrio cholerae*.
This bacterium causes cholera.

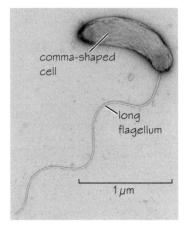

comma-shaped cell

long flagellum

1 μm

(a) Calculate the magnification of the image.

The image of the cell is 25 mm long. Bacteria are usually about 2 μm long.
25 mm = 25 000 μm. Therefore the magnification is $\frac{25\,000}{2}$ = ×12 500

(2 marks)

2 The population of the UK was 8 million in 1832 and reached 65 million by the start of 2017.

(a) Calculate the rate of population growth between 1832 and 2017. Show your working.

Increase in population size = 65 million − 8 million = 57 million
Rate of growth = $\frac{57\ million}{185}$ = 308 108.108 108 people per year

(2 marks)

(1) a In 1(a) the student has recalled that bacteria are usually about 2 μm long and has used this information to calculate the magnification. How should she have calculated the magnification?

....

b Calculate the correct magnification. Look closely at the information provided in the photo.

(2) a In 2(a) the student has missed one line of working in her response. What should she add to the working?

....

b Why would the student not achieve full marks for her answer?   How many decimal places should there be?
Can you have 0.108108 of a person?

....

Your turn!

It is now time to use what you have learned to answer this exam-style question.
Remember to read the question thoroughly, looking for clues.
Make good use of your knowledge from other areas of biology.

Exam-style question

1 The graph shows the growth of a root plotted against time.

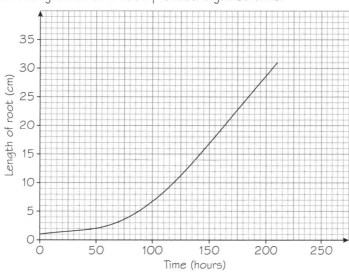

Use a ruler and draw lines on the graph to help you read values accurately.

(a) Give the length of the root at 120 hours.

....

(1 mark)

(b) Calculate the rate of growth of the root between 120 and 150 hours.
Show your working.

Start with .... cm in .... hours. Round your answer to a suitable number of decimal places.

(2 marks)

(c) Calculate the percentage increase in root length between 120 and 180 hours.
Show your working.

- Use the formula:
  percentage change = $\dfrac{\text{actual change}}{\text{original value}} \times 100$
- The original value is the length at 120 hours.
- When something doubles, it increases by 100%.

(3 marks)

Need more practice?

You may be asked to do calculations as part of a question about practical skills, or to analyse a set of data.

Have a go at this exam-style question.

1   The photo shows the lower surface of a leaf.
    The actual size of a guard cell is 0.4 mm
    in length.

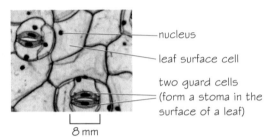

nucleus

leaf surface cell

two guard cells
(form a stoma in the
surface of a leaf)

8 mm

(a)   Calculate the magnification of the photo. Show your working.

(2 marks)

(b)   The guard cells allow oxygen produced in photosynthesis to leave the leaf.

In an investigation, 2.4 cm³ of oxygen was collected over 8 hours.
Calculate the rate of photosynthesis in cm³ oxygen per hour.

(2 marks)

(c)   When the light intensity was increased, the volume of oxygen released in 8 hours
increased to 7.2 cm³. Calculate the percentage increase in the volume of oxygen released.

(3 marks)

Boost your grade

Magnification calculations will usually be about specimens and microscope photographs.
You may be asked to do rate calculations in questions about photosynthesis practicals,
respiration, transpiration, bacterial growth, digestion or diffusion.
Percentage change calculations will often be to do with population size or health and disease.

How confident do you feel about each of these **skills?** Colour in the bars.

1 How do I calculate
   magnification?

2 How do I calculate the
   rate of reaction?

3 How do I calculate a
   percentage?

(7) Answering extended response questions

This unit will help you to answer extended response questions by deciding what is being asked and then planning a concise answer with the right amount of detail.

In the exam, you will be asked to tackle questions such as the one below.

Exam-style question

1   Coronary heart disease can narrow the coronary arteries and reduce blood flow to the heart muscle.

Damage to artery lining due to high blood pressure or substances in tobacco smoke

Fat builds up in the artery wall at the site of damage, making the artery narrower.

A blood clot may block the artery here, or break off and block an artery in another part of the body – causing a heart attack or stroke.

Evaluate the different ways of treating coronary heart disease.

....   (6 marks)

You will already have written some answers to extended response questions. Before starting the **skills boosts**, rate your confidence in your ability to understand, plan and write with the correct amount of detail the answer to an extended response question. Colour in (✏) the bars.

1. **How do I know what the question is asking me to do?**

2. **How do I plan my answer?**

3. **How do I choose the right detail to answer the question concisely?**

The marks given for an extended response question depend both on the level of understanding shown in your answer and on how well your answer is organised.

It is essential to answer the question fully. To do this you need to look for:

- the command word
- the main topic within biology
- what aspect of the topic is being tested
- what information is supplied in diagrams and graphs.

The **command word** usually comes at the start of the question. It tells you what to do.
Here are some common command words.

- Evaluate — use the information supplied, as well as your knowledge and understanding, to consider evidence for and against
- Plan — write a method
- Explain — give the reasons for something happening
- Describe — recall some facts, an event or a process in an accurate way
- Compare — describe the similarities and/or differences between things, not just write about one thing

(1) Two students (**A** and **B**) answer the following question.

Exam-style question

Explain why enzymes work more quickly when they are warm.

.... (3 marks)

A
> At high temperatures enzymes work more quickly but the molecules denature when it gets too hot.

B
> Warmer temperatures give the molecules more kinetic energy so they move more quickly and collide more often.

(a) Circle Ⓐ the command word in the exam-style question.

(b) Tick ✓ the answer you think is better.

(c) Highlight ✐ the part of the answer that you have ticked that contains the explanation.

(2) Two students (**C** and **D**) answer the following question.

Exam-style question

Compare natural selection and artificial selection.

.... (6 marks)

C
> Natural selection is selection by the environment. Individuals that are better adapted are more likely to survive and pass on their genes. The next generation are more likely to have the good adaptations. In artificial selection man selects the individuals that reproduce. It is a much quicker process as the non-adapted individuals do not breed.

D
> Selection involves the choice of breeding partners. When farmers do this it is called artificial selection. Individuals with good adaptations breed to pass these adaptations on to their offspring so that the next generation is well adapted. This means that the population gets better and better adapted to the conditions.

(3) (a) Look at the exam-style question. What does the command word 'compare' mean? ✐

....

(b) Highlight ✐ three words or phrases of that make answer **C** a better comparison than **D**.

How do I know what the question is asking me to do?

To understand what the question is asking you to do you must:
- recognise and understand the command word
- identify the topic being tested and what aspect of the topic you are being asked to write about.

(1) Circle (A) the command word in these questions:

(a) Describe the effect of ....

(b) Explain the role of predators in ....

(c) Draw a fully labelled diagram of a leaf.

(d) Calculate the rate of decomposition.

Exam-style question

1 There are many factors that contribute to the risk of developing coronary heart disease (CHD). The diagram shows how CHD can develop.

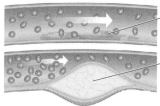

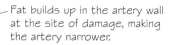

Damage to artery lining due to high blood pressure or substances in tobacco smoke

Fat builds up in the artery wall at the site of damage, making the artery narrower.

A blood clot may block the artery here, or break off and block an artery in another part of the body – causing a heart attack or stroke.

Being obese and smoking cigarettes are risk factors for developing CHD.

(a) Explain how being obese and smoking cigarettes increases the probability that a person will develop CHD.

.... (6 marks)

---

(2) Read the exam-style question above carefully and analyse it by answering these questions.

(a) Circle (A) the **command word**.

(b) Circle (A) the word or words that tell you the **main topic** in biology that is being tested.

(c) Underline (A) the **aspects of this topic** that are being tested.

(d) Highlight (✐) any **useful information** in the question and on the diagram.

Exam-style question

2 Catalase is an enzyme found in many plant and animal tissues. It catalyses the decomposition of hydrogen peroxide to water and oxygen gas: $2H_2O_2 \rightarrow 2H_2O + O_2$

The oxygen gas can be collected by displacing water in an upturned test tube.

(a) Describe how you would test a range of tissues for catalase activity and how you would ensure it is a fair test.

.... (6 marks)

---

(3) (a) Circle (A) the **command word** in the exam-style question above.

(b) Circle (A) the word or words that tell you the **main topic** in biology that is being tested.

(c) Underline (A) the **aspects of this topic** that are being tested in this question.

(d) Highlight (✐) any **useful information** in the question.

Biology

② How do I plan my answer?

Planning your answer is very important. First, think through the topic carefully and decide which parts of the topic are relevant to the question. Then consider the order in which points should be included.

Exam-style question

1 Homeostasis involves the maintenance of internal conditions such as temperature, pH and blood glucose concentration.

(a) Explain why temperature and pH need to be kept constant in the body and what may happen if levels change too far from the optimum.

.... (6 marks)

① Circle Ⓐ the command word in the exam-style question above.   What am I being asked about?

You are told that temperature, pH and blood glucose concentration are controlled in homeostasis.

② Write ✐ the two factors you need to focus on.   What do I know about this topic?

You should know a lot about how temperature and pH can affect the rate of reactions.

The first step is to recall what you can about enzyme activity. Below are the things a student jotted down about enzymes. They have underlined what they think is relevant to the exam-style question.

• Enzymes are proteins	☐	• <u>Enzymes speed up (catalyse) chemical reactions</u> 3	☐
• Enzymes have an active site	☐	• Enzymes work best at a particular pH called the optimum pH	☐
• At very high or low pH most enzymes are inactive	☐	• At low temperatures enzyme activity is low	☐
• The active site is denatured by high temperature	☐	• As temperature rises activity increases	☐
• Extremes of pH will alter the shape of the active site	☐	• This is because the enzyme molecules have more kinetic energy and collide more often	☐
• Proteases digest proteins, lipase digests fats and amylase is found in saliva and it digests starch	☐	• <u>Chemical reactions in the cell need enzymes to work quickly</u> 2	☐
• <u>Some enzymes act inside cells and others act outside cells</u> 1	☐		

③ ⓐ Highlight ✐ the statements that explain the effect of temperature on enzyme activity.

ⓑ Circle Ⓐ the statements that explain the effect of pH on enzyme activity.

The student has numbered the general statements about enzymes to show a possible order.

④ ⓐ Write ✐ numbers on the plan to show what order you would write the statements about temperature.

ⓑ Write ✐ numbers on the plan to show what order you would write the statements about pH.

3 How do I choose the right detail to answer the question concisely?

You can get the right amount of detail in your answer by:
- selecting the parts of the whole topic that answer the question
- referring back to the command word to see the style you should use in your answer.

Exam-style question

1 In the early part of the twentieth century wolves were hunted and removed from the Kaibab Plateau in Arizona. The result was a rapid increase in the deer population followed by a collapse in the deer population a few years later. Scientists noted that all the trees had been stripped of leaves.

The table shows the size of the deer population on the plateau between 1900 and 1940.

Year	1900	1905	1910	1915	1920	1924	1926	1930	1940
Deer population	4000	4000	10000	24000	65000	100000	40000	20000	10000

(a) Explain why the population of deer increased and then decreased so quickly.

.... (6 marks)

(1) What does the command word 'explain' mean? ✏ ....

....

You must include anything you can recall that can help with your explanation. Here the population of deer rises and then falls. Think about what factors could make that happen.

Here are some student notes on the information in the table and what they already know may cause populations to rise and fall.

A The deer population was constant before the wolves were removed. ☐

B The deer population started to increase slowly, but the increase got quicker and quicker.
In 1926 the population size suddenly fell. ☐

C Wolves eat enough deer to limit the size of the deer population. ☐

D Wolves are predators that eat deer. ☐

E The population starved. ☐

F The deer ate all the leaves from the trees so that there was no more food left. ☐

G When the wolves were removed the deer could breed more quickly. ☐

(2) (a) Highlight ✏ the statements that help to **explain** the rise and fall of the deer population.

(b) Number ✏ the statements in the order you would use them in your answer.

If you can put the word 'because' in front of a statement, then it is probably an explanation.

Biology

Sample response

Extended response questions can cover any topic. Read the question carefully, use your knowledge and plan your response.

Exam-style question

1 Microbial growth can be reduced by using antibiotics or antibacterial chemicals such as bleach, by reducing the pH or by reducing the temperature.

(a) Evaluate each method as a way of preserving fresh meat for human consumption, making clear which method is best.

.... **(6 marks)**

Here is one student's response to the exam-style question above.

> In the right conditions bacteria can grow quickly – doubling their population every 20–30 minutes. As they grow they take nutrients from their surroundings – if this is in a human they cause disease. Antibiotics such as penicillin can be used to kill the bacteria and cure the disease. However, antibiotics only kill bacteria so diseases caused by fungi and viruses are not cured. The growth of microbes can be reduced by changing the pH. When food is treated it is called pickling, but pickling would alter the taste of the meat. Another way to keep the food fresh would be salting or covering in sugar like jam. But this would give you sweet tasting meat. Meat is usually kept in the freezer or fridge. The coolness stops the microbes growing but also keeps the meat fresh without affecting the taste. This would be the best way to keep the meat as it does not alter the taste.

(1) The command word is 'evaluate'. Has the response successfully answered the question?

Circle Ⓐ your opinion. **Yes / No**   What did the question ask?

(2) Underline Ⓐ a sentence or phrase in the response that shows the student has evaluated the benefits and risks associated with one method of preservation.

(3) Has the student made clear which is the best method of preservation?

Circle Ⓐ your opinion. **Yes / No**   Is the response well planned?

(4) Have all aspects of the question been considered? Circle Ⓐ your opinion. **Yes / No**

If not, write ✏ what has been missed.

....

....

(5) Does the response have a logical sequence of statements?
Circle Ⓐ your opinion. **Yes / No**   Has the student selected the
                                                                right detail for a concise answer?

Write ✏ how the sequence could be improved.

....

....

Your turn!

It is now time to use what you have learned to answer this exam-style question.
Remember to read the question thoroughly, looking for clues.
Make good use of your knowledge from other areas of biology.

Read the exam-style question and answer it using the guided steps below.

Exam-style question

1   Coronary heart disease can narrow the coronary arteries and reduce blood flow to
    the heart muscle.

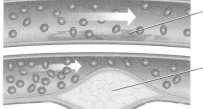

Damage to artery lining
due to high blood pressure
or substances in tobacco smoke

Fat builds up in the artery wall
at the site of damage, making
the artery narrower.

A blood clot may block the artery
here, or break off and block an
artery in another part of the body
– causing a heart attack or stroke.

   (a)   Evaluate the different ways of treating coronary heart disease.

.... **(6 marks)**

(1)   Circle (A) the command word.

(2)   What is the disease to be treated? (✏) ....

(3)   On paper, copy and complete (✏) the table to answer the following questions:

   a   What different types of treatment are there?

   b   What are the benefits of each type of treatment?

   c   What are the risks associated with each type of treatment?

Treatment	Benefit	Risk

(4)   Now decide on the order. Should you list all the benefits of all the treatments before listing any
    risks, or would it be better to list the benefits and risks of each treatment together?
    Write down (✏) your ideas.

....

....

....

(5)   Write (✏) your own answer to the question on a separate piece of paper.

Need more practice?

In the exam, questions about movement into and out of cells could occur as:
- simple standalone questions
- part of a question on how cells, tissues and organs work in plants and animals
- part of a question about a practical test

An extended response question could cover any topic. Use this checklist to help you mark your answer to the exam-style question on page 55.

Checklist	
What did the question ask?	✓
Have you identified the main topic being tested?	
Have you written about the right aspect of the topic tested?	
Does your response answer the command word (evaluate)?	
Is the response well planned?	
Have you discussed all aspects of the question?	
Have you sequenced your statements effectively?	
Have you selected the right detail for a concise answer?	
Have you included any information that is not relevant?	
Is your answer as concise as it could be?	

You can also use this checklist to review your answer to the exam-style question below.

On paper, have a go at this exam-style question.

Exam-style question

1   There are many factors that affect the rate of photosynthesis. These include light intensity, temperature and carbon dioxide concentration.

(a)   Plan an experiment to investigate the effect of light intensity on the rate of photosynthesis in pondweed, an aquatic plant.

(6 marks)

Boost your grade

Ensure you know the meanings of all the command words used for exam questions. Practise making your answers relevant by picking a question from a past paper and writing the four most important points about the topic.

How confident do you feel about each of these **skills?** Colour in the bars.

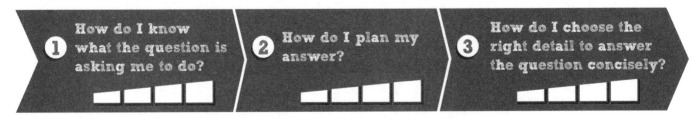

1 How do I know what the question is asking me to do?

2 How do I plan my answer?

3 How do I choose the right detail to answer the question concisely?

① Structure, bonding and the properties of substances

This unit will help you to explain the properties of substances, by using the correct terms to describe the structure and bonding in those substances.

In the exam, you will be asked to tackle questions such as the one below.

Exam-style question

1   Magnesium chloride is an ionic compound and has a high melting point.

Explain why magnesium chloride has a high melting point.

.... (3 marks)

You will already have done some work on structure, bonding and the properties of substances. Before starting the **skills boosts**, rate your confidence in each area. Colour in ✏ the bars.

① How do I explain how ions are formed?

② How do I draw dot-and-cross diagrams to explain how ionic bonds are formed?

③ How do I explain the properties of ionic compounds?

Chemistry

First, make sure you understand the terms atom, ion and molecule.

- Atoms, ions and molecules are all examples of particles.
- Elements are made up of **atoms**. An atom has a nucleus that contains protons and neutrons. The nucleus is surrounded by electrons in shells.
- An **ion** is an atom or group of atoms with a positive or negative charge.
- A **molecule** is a group of atoms bonded together.

> **Remember** Atoms have no overall charge, as the number of protons (+) is **the same** as the number of electrons (−).

① Draw ✎ lines to link each particle with the correct statement(s). You may find that some particles can be linked to more than one statement and some statements match with more than one particle. One link has been done for you.

Particle	Statement
	An atom or group of atoms with a positive or negative charge
Atom	Contains protons and neutrons in the nucleus
	Formed when metals react with non-metals
Ion	Two or more atoms joined together by covalent bonds
	Formed when an atom loses or gains electrons
Molecule	Formed when non-metals react with non-metals

② Complete ✎ these sentences to say what type of particles are formed when magnesium and oxygen react together.

Magnesium is a .... and .... is a non-metal. ....
atoms will react with oxygen .... to form .... ions and oxide ions.

③ What type of particles are formed when the following elements react together? ✎

> Keep your periodic table handy to check if the element is a metal or a non-metal.

a sodium and chlorine

....

....

b carbon and oxygen

....

....

1 How do I explain how ions are formed?

Atoms are more stable if they have a full outer electron shell, like a noble gas. An atom can achieve a full outer shell by gaining or losing electrons and becoming an **ion**. Metal atoms tend to **lose electrons** and form **positive ions**. Non-metal atoms tend to **gain electrons** and form **negative ions**.

1 A student has written the electronic configurations for some elements.

The **electronic configuration** shows the arrangement of electrons in the shells.

a Tick ✓ the correct answers and correct ✎ any mistakes.

Element	Electronic configuration	✓	Correction
lithium (Z = 3)	2.1		
fluorine (Z = 9)	2.6		
aluminium (Z = 13)	2.8.3		
calcium (Z = 20)	2.8.8		

The atomic number (Z) tells you the number of protons in an atom of an element. The number of electrons is the same as the number of protons because an atom has no charge.

b State ✎ which of the elements in a will form negative ions. Explain your answer in terms of electrons.

Which atoms will need to gain electrons to have a full outer shell?

....

....

A sodium atom (2.8.1) loses **one** electron to become a sodium ion (2.8). The sodium ion has a full outer shell of electrons. The table shows how to work out the charge on the ion.

	Number of protons (and their charge)	Number of electrons (and their charge)	Overall charge	Symbol
Sodium atom (Z = 11)	11 (+11)	11 (−11)	0	Na
Sodium ion	11 (+11)	10 (−10)	+1	Na^+

2 Complete ✎ the table below.

	Number of protons (and their charge)	Number of electrons (and their charge)	Overall charge	Symbol
Chlorine atom (Z = 17)	17 (...........)	....	....	....
Chloride ion	....	18 (...........)	....	....
Magnesium atom (Z = 12)	....	....	0	....
Magnesium ion	....	....	....	Mg^{2+}

3 a A sodium ion is represented as Na^+ and has an electronic configuration of (2.8). Explain, in terms of electrons, how a potassium ion is formed from a potassium atom (Z = 19). ✎

....

....

b Write ✎ the formula and electronic configuration for a potassium ion.

....

Chemistry Unit 1 Structure, bonding and the properties of substances   59

Chemistry

2 How do I draw dot-and-cross diagrams to explain how ionic bonds are formed?

Dot-and-cross diagrams are used to show what happens to the electrons when bonds are formed.

What is an ionic bond?

An ionic bond is formed by the transfer of electrons between atoms to produce positive and negative ions. The strong force of attraction between the oppositely charged ions is an ionic bond.

Sodium reacts with chlorine to form sodium chloride.

When non-metals react to form negative ions, the end of the name changes to -ide. For example, a chlorine atom becomes a chloride ion.

1 a Write ✐ the electronic configuration for an atom of sodium (Z = 11) and an atom of chlorine (Z = 17). Then draw dot-and-cross diagrams of the atoms. Sodium has been done for you.

Dots show electrons from one atom and crosses show electrons from the other atom. The electrons themselves are all identical.

Sodium

electronic configuration ....

Chlorine

electronic configuration ....

b Now write ✐ the electronic configuration and draw dot-and-cross diagrams for sodium and chloride ions.
Sodium has been done for you.

Sodium ion

electronic configuration ....$[2.8]^+$............

Chloride ion

electronic configuration ....

2 Draw ✐ dot-and-cross diagrams to show the ions formed when lithium reacts with fluorine to form lithium fluoride. Include the electronic configuration and the charges on the ions.

Remember The strong electrostatic force of attraction between the ions is known as an ionic bond.

Lithium ion

electronic configuration ....

Fluoride ion

electronic configuration ....

3 How do I explain the properties of ionic compounds?

When you explain the properties of ionic compounds, start by looking at the structure and bonding and then explain how they affect the properties.

Melting points and boiling points

- Ionic bonds are very strong so a lot of energy is needed to break them, to separate the ions.
- Ionic compounds form a giant lattice which contains many of these strong bonds, so they have high melting and boiling points.

(1) Which of the following compounds are likely to be ionic? Tick ✓ your choice(s).

A Melting point is 800 °C

B Melting point is 150 °C

C Melting point is 2852 °C

> Ionic compounds have high melting points. Look for values above 150 °C.

Electrical conductivity

- Ionic compounds conduct electricity when they are dissolved in water or when they are melted. This is because their ions are free to move and carry the current.
- However, ionic compounds do not conduct electricity when they are solid. This is because their ions cannot move around in the lattice structure.

(2) The table shows the properties of four compounds.

Compound	Melting point (°C)	Conducts electricity when solid?	Conducts electricity when molten?
W	805	no	yes
X	2064	yes	yes
Y	762	no	yes
Z	120	no	no

a Identify the compound(s) that have ionic bonding.

> Think about the strong bonds and the energy needed to separate the ions

....

b Explain your answers to a.

....

....

....

....

....

Sample response

To answer exam questions about ionic compounds, you need to:
- learn and use the correct terms for the different particles
- work out how many electrons are lost or gained
- explain how ions are formed.

Exam-style questions

1 Which of the following is the symbol for a cation?

A ☒ O^{2-} B ☒ H_2O C ☒ K^+ D ☒ Ca (1 mark)

2 Magnesium oxide is an ionic compound. The electronic configuration of magnesium is 2.8.2. The electronic configuration of oxygen is 2.6.

Describe, in terms of electrons, how a magnesium atom and an oxygen atom form ions in magnesium oxide, MgO.

.... (3 marks)

(1) The student chose Ca. This is incorrect.

a Give ✎ the correct answer.

A cation is a positively charged ion.

....

b Suggest ✎ a reason for the mistake they have made.

You need to be able to recognise atoms, ions and molecules from their symbols and formulae.

....

....

Use these example student responses to help you to answer question 2.

A | *Magnesium atoms lose and oxygen atoms gain, to form ions.*

B | *When magnesium oxide is formed, a magnesium atom loses two electrons and an oxygen atom gains two electrons, to form magnesium ions, Mg^{2+}, and oxide ions, O^{2-}. The two electrons are transferred from a magnesium atom to an oxygen atom.*

The words highlighted in question 2 give you useful information. Use this information to prompt your thinking and help you answer the question.

Remember The number of electrons lost or gained depends on the number of electrons in the outer shell.

(2) a Which student response would gain more marks: **A** or **B**? Circle Ⓐ your answer.

b Write ✎ **two** reasons why this answer would gain more marks.

....

....

....

....

....

Your turn!

It is now time to use what you have learned to answer the question below. Remember to read the question thoroughly, looking for clues. Make good use of your knowledge from other areas of chemistry.

Read the exam-style question and answer it using the guided steps below.

Exam-style question

1   Magnesium chloride is an ionic compound and has a high melting point.

Explain why magnesium chloride has a high melting point.

.... (3 marks)

Before answering this question, think about the following points.

1   What does the **command** word in the question mean?

....

2   Think about the structure and bonding. Answer the following questions.

   a   Is magnesium chloride formed from a metal and a non-metal?

   ....

   b   Do the atoms lose, gain or share electrons?

   ....

   You need to use electronic configurations here.

   c   Will the elements form an ionic compound or a covalent compound?

   ....

   d   What forces of attraction will be holding the structure together?

   Think about the particles. Are they charged? What holds them together? Will a lot of energy be required to separate them?

   ....

   e   What type of structure will the compound form?

   ....

3   Now answer the question in full.

....

....

....

....

....

....

....

Chemistry

Need more practice?

In the exam, questions about structure, bonding and the properties of substances could occur as:

- simple standalone questions
- part of a question on the properties of different types of substance
- part of a question about a practical test.

Have a go at this exam-style question.

Exam-style question

1 Sodium chloride is an ionic substance. It is a crystalline solid at room temperature. It has a high melting point. It conducts electricity when molten and when in aqueous solution.

Explain the properties of sodium chloride. Refer to the particles present and the forces between them.

....

....

....

....

....

....

....

....

....

....

....

(4 marks)

Boost your grade

To improve your grade, you need to be able to:

- explain why covalent compounds are poor conductors of electricity
- explain the properties and uses of diamond and graphite in terms of their structure and bonding.

How confident do you feel about each of these **skills?** Colour in ✐ the bars.

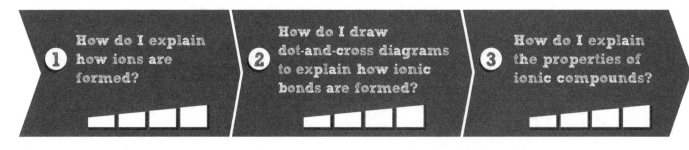

1 How do I explain how ions are formed?

2 How do I draw dot-and-cross diagrams to explain how ionic bonds are formed?

3 How do I explain the properties of ionic compounds?

② Preparing soluble salts

This unit will help you to write a method for preparing soluble salts. You will also learn how to suggest improvements to a method.

In the exam, you will be asked to tackle questions such as the one below.

Exam-style question

1   Soluble salts of metals can be made by reacting an acid with an insoluble metal compound.

Plan an experiment to prepare pure, dry crystals of copper chloride, $CuCl_2$, by reacting a suitable copper compound with a suitable acid.

You may use equations if you wish.

....   (6 marks)

You will already have done some work on improving methods for preparing salts during your practical work. Before starting the **skills boosts**, rate your confidence in planning methods for preparing salts. Colour in ✏ the bars.

1 How do I decide on the method to be used to prepare a soluble salt?

2 How do I describe the method used to prepare a soluble salt?

3 How can I improve a method used to prepare a salt?

To prepare a soluble salt, you need to know the chemical reactions that will produce a salt. Use the name of the salt to work out the correct chemicals to use to make it.

- An **acid** is a substance with a pH of less than 7. Examples are nitric acid, hydrochloric acid and sulfuric acid.
- A **base** is a substance which reacts with an acid, neutralising the acid, and makes a salt and water. Examples are copper oxide, sodium hydroxide and calcium carbonate.
- An **alkali** is a base that dissolves in water. This means that all alkalis are bases. Examples are sodium hydroxide and potassium hydroxide.

Here are some examples of **neutralisation** reactions:

acid + metal oxide ⟶ salt + water

acid + metal carbonate ⟶ salt + water + carbon dioxide

acid + metal hydroxide ⟶ salt + water

When a metal carbonate reacts with an acid, carbon dioxide is also produced.

① Here is a word equation for an acid reacting with a base:

sulfuric acid + copper oxide ⟶ copper sulfate + water

Look at the equation. Now write 🖉 the following:

Remember A base can be a metal oxide, a metal hydroxide or a metal carbonate.

a the acid is ....

b the base is ....

c the salt is ....

Salts are made up of a positive metal ion and a negative ion from the acid.

Here are some examples:

- a copper salt could come from copper oxide
- a sodium salt could come from sodium hydroxide
- sulfuric acid produces sulfate salts
- hydrochloric acid produces chloride salts
- nitric acid produces nitrate salts.

② A student has given incorrect names for the salts produced in some reactions.

Circle Ⓐ the part of the name that is incorrect for each salt. Then write 🖉 the complete correct name for each salt.

a magnesium oxide + sulfuric acid ⟶ magnesium chloride

....

b copper oxide + hydrochloric acid ⟶ copper nitrate

....

c sodium hydroxide + nitric acid ⟶ potassium nitrate

....

1 How do I decide on the method to be used to prepare a soluble salt?

There are two things to think about when preparing a soluble salt.
- Which reactants will you use to prepare the named salt (which metal compound and which acid)?
- Is the metal compound you are going to use a soluble base (an alkali) or an insoluble base? The answer to this question will tell you which method to use.

(1) You wish to prepare magnesium chloride.

a Circle Ⓐ either **Yes** or **No** in this flow chart to help you decide on the reactants.

Is the metal in the salt a group 1 metal?

Yes —— Group 1 metals form oxides and hydroxides that are **soluble** bases

No —— Other metals, those not in group 1, form **insoluble** bases

Use your periodic table to find the group number.

b Tick ✓ the name of the correct acid to use to prepare magnesium chloride.

- to make a nitrate, use nitric acid
- to make a chloride, use hydrochloric acid
- to make a sulfate, use sulfuric acid

c Write ✎ the names of the acid and base you would use to make magnesium chloride.

acid: ....

base: ....

d Now decide which method to use.

Circle Ⓐ either **Yes** or **No**. Look back at your answer to **a**.

Is the base to be used soluble?	
Yes	No
• Use titration to find volumes of acid and alkali • Repeat with no indicator, adding exact volumes • Evaporate some water and then crystallise	• Add insoluble base to acid, until the base is in excess • Filter off the excess • Evaporate some water and then crystallise

(2) Give ✎ the **reactants** to be used and the **method** needed to prepare these soluble salts. The first one has been done for you.

Is the metal compound you are using a soluble base or an insoluble base?

a potassium sulfate: *reactants: potassium hydroxide (a soluble base) and dilute sulfuric acid*

method: titration, then use the same volumes to react; remove the water to produce crystals

b zinc nitrate: reactants ....

method ....

....

c sodium sulfate: reactants ....

method ....

....

Chemistry

② How do I describe the method used to prepare a soluble salt?

The method should be clear. Include all steps, the chemicals, the apparatus and the techniques used.

As in skills boost 1, you need to decide on the reactants to start with and the method to use.

Now let's think about the **DETAIL** you need to include in your method.

- **D**escribe the steps involved, in the right order.
- **E**quation: write word and chemical equations for the reaction.
- **T**echniques: include the technique to be used at each point in the method.
- **A**pparatus: use the correct names for the pieces of apparatus used.
- **I**magine carrying out your method. Will it work? Will it make the salt?
- **L**ook back at your method, to check you have not missed anything.

① How would you prepare the salt zinc chloride, $ZnCl_2$, from an insoluble base and an acid?

a Write ✎ a **word equation** for the reaction to produce zinc chloride.

Look at the 'Get started' page.
Dilute acids are used to make salts.

....

b Now think about the detail of the method.

Write ✎ a number in each box to put these steps in the correct order.
The first one has been done for you.

A Warm the beaker of acid in a water bath. ☐

B Measure 25 cm³ of dilute hydrochloric acid into a beaker. 1

C Filter the mixture to remove the excess zinc oxide and transfer the filtrate to an evaporating basin. ☐

D Add zinc oxide to the acid and stir. Continue adding zinc oxide until all of the acid has reacted with the zinc oxide and there is an excess. ☐

E Heat the evaporating basin. Stop heating when crystals start to form. ☐

c What were the following pieces of apparatus used for? ✎   Re-read the method in **b**.

Water bath: ....

....

Evaporating basin: ....

....

d Which **two** techniques are included in this method? Tick ✓ **two** boxes.

Evaporation ☐   Distillation ☐   Titration ☐   Filtration ☐

③ How can I improve a method used to prepare a salt?

To improve a method for preparing a salt, you should think about the **detail** of the method.
- Are all of the steps included?
- Are the steps in the right order?
- Are the correct apparatus and techniques used in the method?

Learn the core practical methods. You will then be able to suggest improvements to another given method.

Exam-style question

1   A student prepares the salt magnesium chloride. This is the method used.

   A   Measure $20\,cm^3$ of dilute hydrochloric acid into a beaker.

   B   Add some magnesium oxide powder to the acid.

   C   Heat the solution of the salt until crystals form.

Explain **two** ways of improving this experimental method in order to increase the amount and quality of magnesium chloride that could be obtained from $20\,cm^3$ of dilute hydrochloric acid.

....   (6 marks)

① Is anything missing in the method? Work through steps A, B and C.
Circle Ⓐ **Yes**, **No** or **Don't know** and then write ✎ your ideas.

A Measure $20\,cm^3$ of dilute hydrochloric acid into a beaker.

Has the acid been warmed, to ensure a full reaction? **Yes** / **No** / **Don't know**

What apparatus would you use to heat the acid? ....

....

B Add some magnesium oxide powder to the acid.

Has all of the acid reacted? **Yes** / **No** / **Don't know**

How will you know if all the acid has reacted?

....

If there is an excess of magnesium oxide, has it been removed? **Yes** / **No**

Which technique could you use to remove the excess?

....

C Heat the solution of the salt until crystals form.

Has the water been evaporated off slowly? **Yes** / **No** / **Don't know**

What apparatus would you use?

....

Was the product then left to form crystals? **Yes** / **No** / **Don't know**

How long should you leave the solution? ....

② How could you improve this method so as to increase the amount and quality of the magnesium chloride salt produced? Write ✎ **two** improvements.

1   ....

....

2   ....

....

Chemistry

Sample response

To answer a question about preparing salts, you need to think about:
- the chemical equation for the reaction used to produce the salt
- the apparatus and techniques used to make the salt
- the steps in the method, to see if they are all included and are in the right order.

This method was written by a student. They were asked to make the salt magnesium nitrate from an acid and an insoluble base.

$MgO(s) + H_2SO_4(aq) \longrightarrow MgSO_4(aq) + H_2O(l)$

I will make magnesium nitrate from magnesium oxide and dilute sulfuric acid.

Use a beaker to measure out 25 cm³ of acid. Heat the acid using a Bunsen burner to warm it and then add magnesium oxide to the acid. Filter off the excess magnesium oxide. Add the solution to a beaker and heat it to remove the water.

---

(1) Read the advice in the yellow box then underline Ⓐ the errors in the student's method above.

Think about the **DETAIL** shown in the method.
- Describe the steps involved, in the right order.
- Equation: write word and chemical equations for the reaction.
- Techniques: include the technique used at each point in the method.
- Apparatus: use the correct names for the pieces of apparatus used.
- Imagine carrying out the method. Will it work? Will it make the salt?
- Look back at the method. Has anything been missed out?

(2) List 🖊 the errors. Write 🖊 the correct version.

Errors	Corrections
1	
2	
3	
4	
5	

Your turn!

It is now time to use what you have learned to answer the question below. Remember to read the question thoroughly, looking for clues. Make good use of your knowledge from other areas of chemistry.

Exam-style question

1   Soluble salts of metals can be made by reacting an acid with an insoluble metal compound.

Plan an experiment to prepare pure, dry crystals of copper chloride, $CuCl_2$, by reacting a suitable copper compound with a suitable acid.

You may use equations if you wish.

.... **(6 marks)**

Before you start to write your answer, read through this checklist:

Checklist In my answer I need to consider:	$\checkmark$
COMMAND word: Check to see you are answering the question.	
REACTION: Decide on the chemicals to use to produce the salt.	
APPARATUS: Identify the correct apparatus and equipment to be used.	
METHOD: Are the method steps in the right order?	
PURE and DRY: Will the salt be pure and dry if you use your method?	
EQUATION: Include a chemical equation for the reaction.	
READ your answer through: Is it worth the marks?	

1   Write ✐ your answer to the exam-style question. If you need more space to write your answer, continue on paper.

....
....
....
....
....
....
....
....
....

2   Check your answer against the checklist. Identify ✐ **two** improvements to your plan.

1   ....
....

2   ....
....

Need more practice?

In the exam, questions about preparing salts could occur as:

- simple standalone questions
- part of a question on the reactions of acids
- part of a question about a practical test.

Have a go at these exam-style questions. If you need more space to write your answer, continue on paper.

Exam-style questions

1   The salt magnesium sulfate can be made by reacting magnesium carbonate, $MgCO_3$, with dilute sulfuric acid, H_2SO_4.

Write the balanced equation for this reaction.

....

....   **(2 marks)**

2   Salts of metals can be made by reacting one of the metal's compounds with the appropriate acid.

Devise an experiment to prepare pure, dry crystals of zinc nitrate, $Zn(NO_3)_2$, by reacting a suitable zinc compound with a suitable acid.

You may use equations if you wish.

....

....

....

....

....

....   **(6 marks)**

Boost your grade

To improve your grade:

- learn the solubility rules
- practise planning methods to prepare different soluble salts
- make sure you can write chemical equations for neutralisation reactions.

How confident do you feel about each of these **skills?** Colour in the bars.

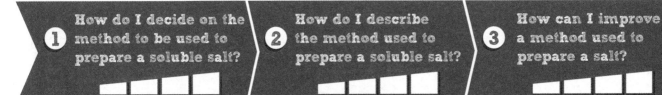

1 How do I decide on the method to be used to prepare a soluble salt?

2 How do I describe the method used to prepare a soluble salt?

3 How can I improve a method used to prepare a salt?

③ Electrolysis

Electrolysis is the decomposition (breakdown) of a compound using electricity. This unit will help you to explain what happens in electrolysis and to predict and explain the products formed during electrolysis.

In the exam, you will be asked to tackle questions such as the one below.

Exam-style question

1   An electrolysis experiment is carried out on different solutions. Electricity is passed through each solution, as shown in Figure 1.

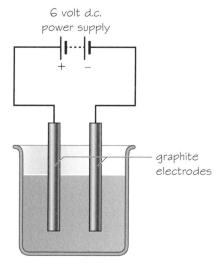

Figure 1

(a) Some of the solutions are electrolytes.

State what is meant by the term **electrolyte**.

.... (2 marks)

(b) When a solution of sodium chloride, NaCl, is electrolysed the products formed at the electrodes are hydrogen and chlorine.

Explain the formation of the products at the electrodes.

.... (4 marks)

You will already have done some work on predicting and explaining the products of electrolysis. Before starting the **skills boosts**, rate your confidence in each area. Colour in 🖉 the bars.

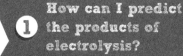
1 How can I predict the products of electrolysis?

2 How do I explain what oxidation and reduction are?

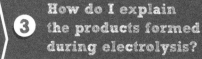
3 How do I explain the products formed during electrolysis?

When you explain why specific products are formed in electrolysis, it is important to use the correct scientific terms in your explanation.

Key terms

- An **ionic compound** is a compound between a metallic element and a non-metallic element.
- An **electrolyte** is an ionic compound that conducts electricity when molten or in aqueous solution. An electrolyte conducts electricity when the ions are able to move.

An aqueous solution is when a solute is dissolved in water.

- **Electrolysis** is the process in which electrical energy, from a direct current supply, decomposes an electrolyte.

Decompose means **to break down.**

(1) Complete 🖉 the following sentences, using words from the box.

conduct	decomposed	electrolysis	melted	move	stop	titration

Molten sodium chloride is .... into sodium and

chlorine by .... Sodium chloride is an ionic

compound. Both molten and aqueous sodium chloride will ....

electricity because the ions are free to ....

Look at Chemistry unit 1 to find out how ions are formed.

Two electrodes are connected to a direct current (d.c.) electricity supply and placed into an electrolyte, as shown in the diagram.

In an ionic compound:

- the metal atoms form positive ions
- the non-metal atoms form negative ions.

During electrolysis, the ions in the electrolyte move towards the electrodes:

- **cations** are positively charged ions and are attracted to the negative **cathode**
- **anions** are negatively charged ions and are attracted to the positive **anode.**

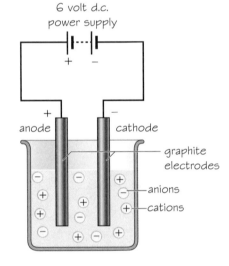

(2) Look at these formulae: K^+ F^- H_2O Cl^- SO_4^{2-} Mg^{2+} CO_2

a Circle Ⓐ the cations in the list of formulae.

b List 🖉 the ions that will be attracted to the anode during electrolysis.

....

(3) Join 🖉 each scientific word to the correct definition.

Electrolyte	A process in which electrical energy, from a direct current, decomposes electrolytes
Electrolysis	To break down a compound into simpler compounds or into elements
Decomposition	An ionic compound which conducts electricity when molten or dissolved in water

1 How can I predict the products of electrolysis?

Salts contain positive metal ions and negative non-metal ions. When a molten salt is electrolysed, ions are **discharged** as atoms or molecules at the electrodes. You can predict the products of electrolysis of any **molten salt**. This is because the salt always decomposes into its elements.

During the electrolysis of **molten** sodium chloride:

- sodium metal is produced at the cathode
- chlorine gas is produced at the anode.

Molten means the salt has been heated until it melts and forms a liquid.

1 Complete ✏ the table below, identifying the products formed during the electrolysis of the **molten salts**. Sodium chloride has been done for you.

	Product at the cathode	Product at the anode
sodium chloride	sodium	chlorine
lead bromide		
potassium iodide		
copper chloride		

2 Predict ✏ the products formed at the cathode and the anode when molten potassium bromide is electrolysed.

Look back at the previous page if you can't remember what happens at each electrode.

   a at cathode: ....

   b at anode: ....

3 Molten sodium chloride can be electrolysed but solid sodium chloride cannot.

   a Are the ions free to move in solid or molten sodium chloride? Circle Ⓐ the correct answer.

> solid   molten

   b Does solid sodium chloride or molten sodium chloride conduct electricity? Circle Ⓐ the correct answer.

> solid   molten

   c Explain ✏ why molten sodium chloride can be electrolysed but solid sodium chloride cannot be electrolysed.

Use the information in **a** and **b** to answer **c**.

....

....

....

....

Chemistry

② How do I explain what oxidation and reduction are?

The words **oxidation** and **reduction** are used to describe the reactions that take place at the electrodes during electrolysis.

① The diagram shows the apparatus used in electrolysis.

Label ✎ the diagram, using the key terms in the box.

Check the meaning of the key terms.

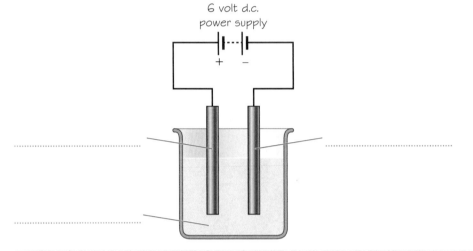

6 volt d.c.
power supply

+ –

anode

cathode

electrolyte

What happens during electrolysis?
* Negative ions, called anions, move to the positive electrode, called the anode.
* At the anode, negative ions lose electrons. Oxidation Is the Loss of electrons.
* Positive ions, called cations, move to the negative electrode, called the cathode.
* At the cathode, positive ions gain electrons. Reduction Is the Gain of electrons.

Remember this imformation using OIL RIG.

② Identify the following reactions as **oxidation** or **reduction** reactions.

Tick ✓ the correct answers.

		oxidation	reduction
a	Copper ions, Cu^{2+}, gain electrons at the cathode, to form copper atoms.	☐	☐
b	Chloride ions, Cl^-, lose electrons at the anode, to form chlorine atoms. Chlorine atoms are bonded together to form chlorine molecules, Cl_2.	☐	☐

③ The reactions at the electrodes can be shown as **half equations**.
* At the **cathode**: $Cu^{2+}(aq) + 2e^- \rightarrow Cu(s)$
* At the **anode**: $2Cl^-(aq) \rightarrow Cl_2 + 2e^-$

e^- is used to show an electron in half equations.

a Where does reduction take place? ✎ ....

b Where does oxidation take place? ✎ ....

c Explain ✎ your answers to **a** and **b** .

....

....

....

....

③ How do I explain the products formed during electrolysis?

To explain the products formed during electrolysis, you need to:
- identify the ions present
- work out the electrodes the ions are attracted to
- explain what happens to the ions at the electrodes.

① Molten potassium chloride is electrolysed.

a List 🖉 the ions present in the electrolyte. ....

b Write 🖉 which ions will be attracted to each electrode.

   i anode ....   **ii** cathode ....

c Write 🖉 the products formed. ....

Water molecules ionise to a very small extent, producing some hydrogen ions, $H^+(aq)$, and hydroxide ions, $OH^-(aq)$. If an ionic compound is dissolved in water, there will be $H^+(aq)$ ions and $OH^-(aq)$ ions as well as the ions from the ionic compound.

② Write 🖉 the four ions present in an aqueous solution of sodium iodide.

....

Learn the following rules to predict the products formed at each electrode during the electrolysis of an aqueous solution.

At the **cathode**	At the **anode**
If the metal is less reactive than hydrogen, the metal will form. For example, copper is less reactive than hydrogen, so copper will form: $$Cu^{2+}(aq) + 2e^- \rightarrow Cu(s)$$	If the negative ion is simple (for example, chloride, Cl^-), the element will form. Chlorine is produced from chloride ions: $$2Cl^-(aq) \rightarrow Cl_2(g) + 2e^-$$
If the metal is more reactive than hydrogen, hydrogen gas will form. For example, sodium is more reactive than hydrogen, so hydrogen forms: $$2H^+(aq) + 2e^- \rightarrow H_2(g)$$	If the negative ion is polyatomic (e.g. sulfate, SO_4^{2-}), oxygen gas will form. If aqueous sodium sulfate is electrolysed, oxygen gas forms: $$4OH^-(aq) \rightarrow 2H_2O(l) + O_2(g) + 4e^-$$

③ Aqueous copper sulfate is electrolysed.

a What forms at the cathode? 🖉

Is copper more or less reactive than hydrogen? You may need to look at the reactivity series to work this out.

....

b What forms at the anode? 🖉

....

④ An aqueous solution of potassium chloride is electrolysed.

a Circle Ⓐ the ions present in the solution.

Remember The H^+ ions and OH^- ions come from the water.

$Br^-(aq)$ $Cl^-(aq)$ $CO_3^{2-}(aq)$ $H^+(aq)$ $I^-(aq)$ $K^+(aq)$ $Li^+(aq)$ $Na^+(aq)$ $OH^-(aq)$ $SO_4^{2-}(aq)$

b Circle Ⓐ the products formed.

$Br_2(l)$ $Cl_2(g)$ $CO_2(g)$ $H_2(g)$ $H_2O(l)$ $I_2(s)$ $K(s)$ $Li(s)$ $Na(s)$

Chemistry

Sample response

In a question about the products formed during the electrolysis of an ionic compound, you need to answer these questions:
- Is the electrolyte molten or in aqueous solution?
- Which ions are present and which electrode will they be attracted to?
- Which ions will lose or gain electrons and which products will be formed?

Exam-style question

1 When a solution of copper sulfate, $CuSO_4$, is electrolysed, the products formed at the electrodes are copper and oxygen.

   Explain the formation of the products at the electrodes. **(4 marks)**

(**1**) Look at the student answer to the above exam-style question.

> Copper sulfate solution is made of copper ions and sulfate ions. The water also is made up of some hydrogen ions and hydroxide ions. The copper (Cu^{2+}) ions and hydrogen ions (H^+) are attracted to the cathode, where copper atoms are formed. The sulfate ions (SO_4^{2-}) and hydroxide ions (OH^-) are attracted to the anode, where oxygen molecules are formed.

☐ / 4

a Using the mark scheme shown below, decide how many marks you would award this answer.

Mark scheme

- Hydrogen (H^+) and copper (Cu^{2+}) ions are attracted to the cathode, and hydroxide (OH^-) ions and sulfate (SO_4^{2-}) ions are attracted to the anode   (1 mark)

- because the ions are attracted to the oppositely charged electrode   (1 mark)

- 1 copper ion accepts 2 electrons to form a copper atom, Cu   (1 mark)

- 4 hydroxide ions (4 OH^-) lose 4 electrons to form an oxygen molecule (O_2)   (1 mark)

b How could this student answer be improved to gain more marks? ✏

....

....

....

(**2**) Now write ✏ your own answer to the exam-style question.

Explain means you need to say how or why something happens. Make sure your answer contains some reasoning.

....

....

....

....

....

....

Your turn!

It is now time to use what you have learned to answer the question below. Remember to read the question thoroughly, looking for clues. Make good use of your knowledge from other areas of chemistry.

Read the exam style question and answer it using the guided steps below.

Exam-style question

1   An electrolysis experiment is carried out on different solutions. Electricity is passed through each solution, as shown in Figure 1.

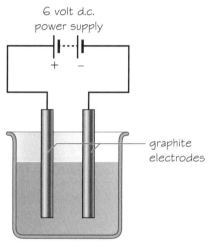

6 volt d.c.
power supply

+   −

graphite
electrodes

Figure 1

(a) Some of the solutions are electrolytes. State what is meant by the term **electrolyte**. (2 marks)

(b) When a solution of sodium chloride, NaCl, is electrolysed the products formed at the electrodes are hydrogen and chlorine.

Explain the formation of the products at the electrodes.   (4 marks)

1 **a** Write ✏ your answer to part (a).   **State** means recall one or more pieces of information.

....

....

b **i** Highlight ✏ the key words.   **Explain** means to say how or why something happens.

What do these words tell you?

• solution: Are the ions free to move? The solute is dissolved in water. Some water is ionised.

• hydrogen: Why is sodium not a product? What happens to the ions?

ii Now answer ✏ part (b) here.   Note that there are 4 marks for this part of the question.

....

....

....

....

Chemistry

Need more practice?

In the exam, questions about electrolysis could occur as:
- simple standalone questions
- part of a question that includes calculations relating to the mass of the products formed
- part of a question about a practical test.

Have a go at this exam-style question. ✎

Exam-style question

1 An electrolysis experiment is carried out on different solutions, **F**, **G** and **H**.

Any products formed at the electrodes are identified. The results are shown below.

Solution	Does solution conduct electricity?	Product at cathode	Product at anode
F	yes	copper	oxygen
G	no	none	none
H	yes	hydrogen	chlorine

(a) Some of these solutions are electrolytes. Explain which of **F**, **G** and **H** are electrolytes.

....

....

.... **(2 marks)**

(b) When a solution of potassium sulfate, K_2SO_4, is electrolysed, the products formed at the electrodes are hydrogen and oxygen.

Explain the formation of the products at the electrodes.

....

....

....

.... **(4 marks)**

Boost your grade

To improve your grade, practise writing half equations for the reactions at the electrodes.
The reactivity series will tell you if a metal is more or less reactive than hydrogen. This will help you to predict the products formed during the electrolysis of aqueous solutions.

How confident do you feel about each of these **skills?** Colour in ✎ the bars.

1 How can I predict the products of electrolysis?

2 How do I explain what oxidation and reduction are?

3 How do I explain the products formed during electrolysis?

④ Rates of reaction

This unit will help you to explain the effect of changing different variables on the rate of reaction. It will also help you to use data from a graph to calculate the rate of reaction.

In the exam, you will be asked to tackle questions such as the one below.

Exam-style question

1   A student investigates the reaction between calcium carbonate and dilute hydrochloric acid. She carries out the reaction with a low concentration of hydrochloric acid and then with a high concentration. She measures the volume of gas over time for each concentration. She plots the graph shown in Figure 1.

Volume of gas produced for different concentrations of acid

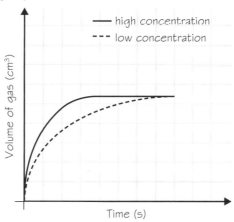

Figure 1

(a) Use the graph to explain which reaction has the fastest rate.

.... (2 marks)

(b) State what the student can conclude about the effect of increasing concentration on the rate of reaction.

.... (2 marks)

(c) Another student finds that increasing the temperature speeds up the reaction. Explain why, using ideas about particles.

.... (3 marks)

You will already have done some work on rates of reaction. Before starting the **skills boosts**, rate your confidence in each area. Colour in the bars.

1   **How do I explain what affects the rate of a reaction?**

2   **How do I investigate the rate of a reaction?**

3   **How do I work out the rate of a reaction?**

Different reactions can happen at different rates. Reactions that happen slowly have a low rate of reaction. An example is iron rusting. Reactions that happen quickly have a high rate of reaction. An example is an explosion.

The chart below shows what happens when a chemical reaction takes place.

1 All substances are made of **particles**. These particles may be atoms, molecules or ions. Chemical reactions take place when reacting particles **collide** with enough energy to react.

2 The minimum amount of energy needed for a reaction to occur is called the **activation energy**.

4 The rate of a reaction depends on the **frequency** of **successful collisions** between reactant particles. The more successful collisions there are, the faster the rate of reaction.

3 Collisions between particles are successful if there is enough energy to **break the bonds**. The atoms can rearrange to form the products of the reaction.

(1) Draw ✏ diagrams to show the **particles** for the following examples.

Use circles of different colours to show different particles. Use curved 'zoom' lines around the particles to show they are moving fast. One diagram has been done for you.

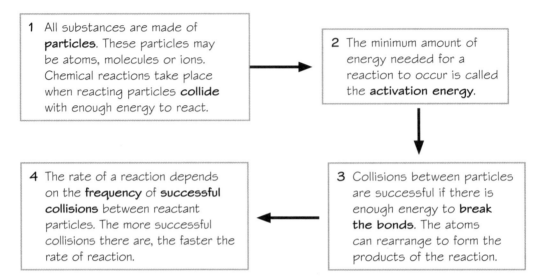

a	b	c	d
Low concentration	High concentration	High temperature	Low temperature

Which conditions produce the fastest reactions? Think about why.

(2) Explain ✏ what will happen if particles collide but they **do not** have the energy needed to react.

....

....

....

(3) Explain ✏ why a lighted splint is needed to light the gas in a Bunsen burner.

Think about what is needed for particles to react.

....

....

....

How do I explain what affects the rate of a reaction?

To explain how changing different variables affects the rate of a reaction, you need to think about what the change will do to the particles involved in the reaction.

Look at these diagrams, showing the particles of a solid as a large lump and in smaller pieces.

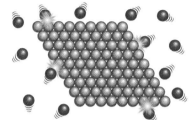
large lump of solid

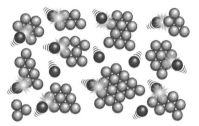
smaller pieces of solid

Increasing the **surface area to volume** ratio of a solid, by decreasing the size of the pieces, increases the rate of reaction. This is because there is **more** surface area for collisions to occur on, so the **frequency of collisions** increases.

Remember Frequency of collisions means how many collisions per second.

(1) Identify which of the following will **increase** the rate of reaction.

Tick ✓ the correct answer.

A Increasing the temperature of acid reacting with zinc metal.

B Decreasing the concentration of acid reacting with marble chips.

C Using larger chips of marble when reacting with acid.

Rates of reaction are increased when the frequency of collisions and/or the energy of collisions is increased.

(2) Using ideas about particles, explain ✏ what happens to the rate of reaction between magnesium and dilute hydrochloric acid, when the concentration of the acid is increased. Use words from the box in your answer.

collisions	frequency of collisions	particles	rate of reaction

Remember Concentration is the number of particles in a specific volume.

....

....

....

....

....

....

Chemistry

2 How do I investigate the rate of a reaction?

Investigating the rate of a reaction involves measuring a change in the amount of reactant used up or a change in the amount of product formed over time.

For example, the equation for the reaction between sodium carbonate and dilute hydrochloric acid is:

> sodium carbonate + hydrochloric acid → sodium chloride + water + carbon dioxide

You can investigate the effect of changing the concentration of acid on the rate of reaction by measuring the volume of carbon dioxide gas produced.

- The variable you change is the **independent** variable. Here it is the concentration of acid.
- The variable you measure (because you expect it to change) is the **dependent** variable. Here it is the volume of carbon dioxide gas produced.
- All other variables should be controlled.

① Circle Ⓐ the independent variable and highlight ✏ the dependent variable in each investigation.

a An investigation into the effect of temperature of dilute hydrochloric acid on the time taken for magnesium to react and disappear.

What do you change?
Which variable is this?

b An investigation into the effect of surface area of marble chips (calcium carbonate) on the volume of gas produced in the reaction with dilute sulfuric acid.

What do you measure?
Which variable is this?

② The reaction between sodium thiosulfate solution and dilute hydrochloric acid produces a yellow precipitate of sulfur. You can measure the rate of the reaction by measuring the time taken for a 'cross' drawn on a piece of paper to disappear (hidden by the sulfur precipitate). We can carry out the experiment using hydrochloric acid at different temperatures.

a What is the dependent variable in this investigation? ✏

What is being measured to see if it has changed?

....

b What is the independent variable? ✏

This is the variable you change.

....

c State ✏ one control variable.

Which variables are staying the same?

....

d Look at the results in the table. Explain ✏ how changing the temperature affects the rate of this reaction.

Look for a pattern in the results.

....

....

....

....

Temperature (°C)	Time taken for cross to disappear (s)
25	142
35	70
45	35
55	18

3 How do I work out the rate of a reaction?

We can measure how quickly the reactants are used up or how quickly the products are formed. We can then use this information to calculate the rate of reaction.

$$\text{rate of reaction} = \frac{\text{amount of reactant used up or product formed}}{\text{time taken}}$$

For example, in a reaction, 14.4 cm³ of oxygen gas was produced in the first 8 seconds. The rate of this reaction is:

$$\text{rate} = \frac{\text{amount of product formed}}{\text{time}} = \frac{14.4}{8} = 1.8 \text{ cm}^3/\text{s}$$

Remember Show your working out in calculations. Include the units.

1 A reaction produced 4.5 cm³ of carbon dioxide gas in the first 5.0 seconds. Calculate 🖉 the rate of this reaction.

The time is in seconds, so the units will be cm³/s.

2 A student investigated the rate of reaction between magnesium and dilute hydrochloric acid. The graph shows the student's results for one concentration of hydrochloric acid.

The table shows the student's results when a **higher** concentration of acid was used.

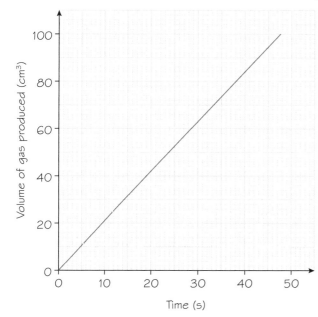

Time (s)	Volume of gas produced (cm³)
0	0
10	35
15	52
20	70
25	85

Remember The steeper the curve, the higher the rate of reaction.

a i Plot 🖉 the results in the table on the grid.

Start at point (0, 0) then point (10, 35) and so on. Use a 'x' to mark each point on the graph.

ii Draw 🖉 a line of best fit through the points you have plotted.

b What is the mean rate of reaction (in cm³/s) in the first 20 seconds, for the **lower** concentration of acid?

Use the graph to find the volume of gas at 20s then use this value in the equation.

Chemistry

Sample response

To answer a question about rates of reaction, you may need to:
- use ideas about particles colliding in your explanations
- apply your practical experience
- plot results onto a graph or calculate the rate of reaction from a given graph.

Look at this exam-style question and student response.

Exam-style question

1 The rate of the reaction between calcium carbonate and dilute hydrochloric acid can be measured when large and small pieces of calcium carbonate are used.
Here is the equation for the reaction.

$$CaCO_3(s) + 2HCl(aq) \rightarrow CaCl_2(aq) + H_2O(l) + CO_2(g)$$

(a) Sketch a graph to show the volume of gas produced against time, for both large and small pieces of calcium carbonate. Label the axes, including the units. Include a title and a key.

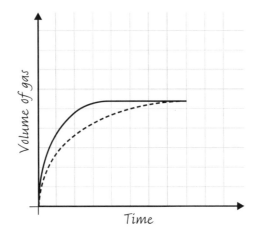

(b) Using ideas about particles, explain how changing the size of the pieces of calcium carbonate affects the rate of the reaction.

Using smaller pieces of calcium carbonate increases the rate of the reaction. This is because

using smaller pieces increases the surface area of the solid, which increases the rate of reaction.

(1) What is missing from the student's sketch graph in part (a)?

Complete ✎ the student's graph.

What should the labels include? How do you know what the graph is telling you?

(2) How can the answer in part (b) be improved?

Write ✎ an improved answer.

Does the answer use the key vocabulary? You need to mention particles, collisions and frequency of collisions.

....

....

....

....

Your turn!

It is now time to use what you have learned to answer the question below. Remember to read the question thoroughly, looking for clues. Make good use of your knowledge from other areas of chemistry.

Exam-style question

1   A student investigates the reaction between calcium carbonate and dilute hydrochloric acid. She carries out the reaction with a low concentration of hydrochloric acid and then with a high concentration. She measures the volume of gas over time for each concentration. She plots the graph shown in Figure 1.

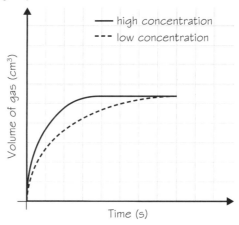

Volume of gas produced for different concentrations of acid

Figure 1

(a) Use the graph to explain which reaction has the fastest rate.

Compare the steepness of the graphs.

....

....

.... (2 marks)

(b) State what the student can conclude about the effect of increasing concentration on the rate of reaction.

Describe what happens as the independent variable is changed.

....

....

.... (2 marks)

(c) Another student finds that increasing the temperature speeds up the reaction.
Explain why, using ideas about particles.

Explain how changing the temperature affects both the frequency of collisions and the energy of the colliding particles.

....

....

....

.... (3 marks)

Need more practice?

In the exam, questions about rates of reaction could occur as:

- simple standalone questions
- part of a question, including calculating the reaction rate from a graph
- part of a question about a practical test.

Have a go at these exam-style questions. If you need more space to write your answer, continue on paper.

Exam-style questions

1   Sodium thiosulfate and dilute hydrochloric acid are both clear, colourless solutions. They react together to form a yellow precipitate of sulfur.

$$2HCl(aq) + Na_2S_2O_3(aq) \rightarrow 2NaCl(aq) + SO_2(g) + S(s) + H_2O(l)$$

State the method you would use to measure the rate of the reaction.

....

....   (2 marks)

2   Figure 1 shows the reaction between marble chips and dilute hydrochloric acid.

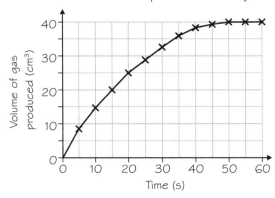

Figure 1

Calculate the mean reaction rate for the first 10 seconds. State the units.

(2 marks)

Boost your grade

To improve your grade, practise plotting graphs of your results for rates of reaction investigations. Also practise calculating the rate of reaction from your graphs.

How confident do you feel about each of these **skills?** Colour in the bars.

1   How do I explain what affects the rate of a reaction?

2   How do I investigate the rate of a reaction?

3   How do I work out the rate of a reaction?

⑤ Chemical calculations

This unit will help you to plan and carry out calculations involving masses in chemistry.

In the exam, you will be asked to tackle questions such as the ones below.

Exam-style questions

1   A student wanted to make 24.0 g of the salt, sodium chloride.

(relative atomic masses: H = 1, C = 12, O = 16, Na = 23, Cl = 35.5)

The equation for the reaction is:

$$Na_2CO_3(s) + 2HCl(aq) \rightarrow 2NaCl(aq) + H_2O(l) + CO_2(g)$$

(a)   The relative formula mass of sodium chloride is 58.5.

Calculate the relative formula mass of sodium carbonate, Na_2CO_3.

.... (1 mark)

(b)   Calculate the mass of sodium carbonate the student should react with dilute hydrochloric acid to make 24.0 g of sodium chloride.

.... (3 marks)

2   A sample of a copper oxide was analysed and found to contain 1.27 g of copper and 0.32 g of oxygen.

Calculate the empirical formula of the copper oxide.

(relative atomic masses: O = 16, Cu = 63.5)

.... (3 marks)

Acids, bases and salts are discussed in Chemistry unit 2.

Chemistry

You will already have done some work on chemical calculations. Before starting the **skills boosts**, rate your confidence in each area. Colour in the bars.

1 How do I set out calculations correctly?

2 How do I calculate empirical formulae?

3 How do I calculate the mass of a reactant or product?

When you calculate a relative formula mass, you use relative atomic masses and chemical formulae.

Relative atomic mass: The mass of an atom is very small. Relative atomic mass (A_r) is a way of comparing the masses of atoms of different elements. The **relative atomic mass** of an element tells you how heavy an atom of that element is, compared with the mass of an atom of carbon-12. Carbon-12 is the standard used for atomic mass and all other atoms are compared with it.

(1) Use your periodic table to write 🖊 the relative atomic masses of the following elements:

a A_r oxygen = ...   **b** A_r calcium = ...   **c** A_r magnesium = ...

(2) How many atoms of helium are needed to equal the mass of one atom of sulfur?   Use your periodic table.

Circle Ⓐ the correct answer. | 1   2   4   8   16   32 |

Isotopes: All atoms of a particular element contain the same number of **protons**. This means the atoms of an element always have the same atomic number. If two atoms have different numbers of protons then they are atoms of different elements.

However, atoms of the same element can contain different numbers of **neutrons**. This will change the mass of the atom. Atoms of the same element with different numbers of neutrons are called **isotopes**.

(3) **a** Which of the following chemical symbols shows an isotope of chlorine?

Tick ✓ the correct box.

A $^{35}_{16}Cl$ ☐   B $^{37}_{17}Cl$ ☐   C $^{36}_{16}Cl$ ☐

b Explain 🖊 your answer to **a**.

....

....

Relative formula mass: The relative formula mass (M_r) is the sum of the relative atomic masses (A_r) of all the atoms or ions in a formula.

Remember

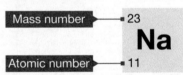
Mass number → 23
Na
Atomic number → 11

(4) Calculate 🖊 the relative formula mass (M_r) of water, H_2O.

(relative atomic masses: H = 1, O = 16)

H_2O has 2 hydrogen, H, atoms and 1 oxygen, O, atom.

relative formula mass = (2 × ....) + (1 × ....) = ...

Start by working out how many atoms there are of each element.

(5) Calculate the relative formula mass of the following compounds. Circle Ⓐ the correct answer.

(relative atomic masses: H = 1, C = 12, O = 16, S = 32)

a carbon dioxide, CO_2 **b** sulfuric acid, H_2SO_4

| 12   28   32   44 | | 49   50   98   194 |

1 How do I set out calculations correctly?

Setting out your answer clearly will help you and the examiner to follow your working, and will help the examiner to see where you have gained marks.

Steps to follow in calculations

1 Identify the information you are given in the question.

2 Explain in words what you are calculating.

3 Substitute in the numbers you know and show your working out.

4 State the units of your answer.

Look at the sample question and student answer below to see how to work through these steps.

> Calculate the relative formula mass (M_r) of magnesium chloride, $MgCl_2$.
> (relative atomic masses: Mg = 24, Cl = 35.5)

1 *The information you are given in the question is the A_r (relative atomic masses) for magnesium and chlorine (24 and 35.5) and the formula of magnesium chloride ($MgCl_2$).*

2 *Magnesium chloride contains 1 atom of Mg and 2 atoms of Cl.*
   The relative formula mass of magnesium chloride = A_r of Mg + (2 × A_r of Cl)

3 *Substituting in the values from the question, M_r magnesium chloride = 24 + (2 × 35.5) = 95*

4 *There are no units, as it is a relative formula mass.*

Now try using the steps to carry out the following calculations.

① Calculate  the relative formula mass (M_r) of iron oxide, Fe_2O_3.

(relative atomic masses: O = 16, Fe = 56)

1 *$A_r(Fe) = 56$, $A_r(O) = 16$, formula is Fe_2O_3* ....

2 ....   The formula shows there
....   are 2 × Fe and 3 × O.

3 ....

4 ....

② Calculate  the relative formula mass (M_r) of calcium hydroxide, $Ca(OH)_2$.

(relative atomic masses: H = 1, O = 16, Ca = 40)

1 ....

2 ....   The brackets in the formula show
....   there are 2 × O and 2 × H.

3 ....

4 ....

Chemistry

2 How do I calculate empirical formulae?

The **empirical formula** is the simplest whole number ratio of atoms or ions of each element in a compound. When you are asked to calculate an empirical formula, you will be
- given the masses of the elements that react together to form a compound
- asked to work out the empirical formula of the compound that is produced.

To do this, you need to find the ratio of the number of atoms of each element reacting together. You will need to know the relative atomic masses of the elements.

Relative atomic masses may be given in the question. If not, you can find them in the periodic table.

(1) Calculate the empirical formula of the compound formed when 0.69 g of sodium reacts with 0.24 g of oxygen.

(relative atomic masses: Na = 23, O = 16)

You may find it helpful to set out your answer in columns, as shown here.

a Complete 🖊 the table below. The first column has been done for you.

	Sodium, Na	Oxygen, O
Mass of each element (g)	0.69	
Divide the mass of each element by the relative atomic mass (A_r) for that element	$\frac{0.69}{23} = 0.03$	$\frac{}{} = 0.02$
Divide the answers by the smaller number to find the simplest whole number ratio	$\frac{0.03}{0.015} = 2$	

You need a column for each element.

Use the masses given in the question.

Look for the smallest number when trying to work out the ratio.

b Write 🖊 the empirical formula of the compound formed. ....

(2) Calculate the empirical formula of the compound formed when 0.24 g of carbon reacts with 0.64 g of oxygen.

(relative atomic masses: C = 12, O = 16)

a Complete 🖊 the table below.

	C	O
Mass of each element (g)		
Divide the mass by the relative atomic mass (A_r) for each element		
Divide the answers by the smaller number to find the simplest whole number ratio		

b Write 🖊 the empirical formula of the compound formed. ....

(3) Calculate 🖊 the empirical formula of the compound formed when 11.2 g of iron reacts with 21.3 g of chlorine.

(relative atomic masses: Cl = 35.5, Fe = 56)

You need to find a whole number ratio.

3 How do I calculate the mass of a reactant or product?

You can use relative atomic masses and balanced chemical equations to calculate the mass of a reactant or a product. The balanced equation tells you that the number of atoms does not change, so the total mass cannot change.

1 Calculate the mass of zinc oxide produced when 13.0 g of zinc completely burns in oxygen.

(relative atomic masses: O = 16, Zn = 65)

$$2Zn(s) + O_2(g) \longrightarrow 2ZnO(s)$$

a Use the A_r values to calculate the relative formula masses, M_r.

Explain in words what you are calculating

relative atomic mass of Zn = 65

relative formula mass of ZnO = (65 × ....) + (................. × ....) = ...

b Use the balanced equation to work out the mass of ZnO produced. Complete the sentences below.

> From the equation, 2Zn gives 2ZnO, so 2 × 65 g of Zn gives
>
> 2 × .... of ZnO. This means that 130 g of Zn gives
>
> .... of ZnO.

Multiply the M_r value for each compound by the number in the equation.

c Use the information from **b** to calculate the mass of ZnO formed from 13 g Zn.

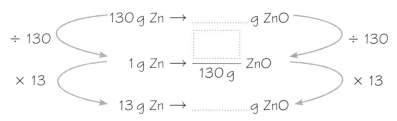

÷ 130   130 g Zn → .... g ZnO   ÷ 130

1 g Zn → $\dfrac{}{130\,g}$ ZnO

× 13   13 g Zn → .... g ZnO   × 13

Dividing by 130 gives 1 g of zinc. Finding the mass for 1 g means you can scale up easily. Multiplying by 13 gives the value in the question.

d State the mass of ZnO. ....

State the units.

2 Calculate the mass of hydrogen produced when 7.2 g of magnesium reacts with dilute hydrochloric acid.

(relative atomic masses: H = 1, Mg = 24, Cl = 35.5)

$$Mg(s) + 2HCl(aq) \longrightarrow MgCl_2(aq) + H_2(g)$$

Which parts of the balanced equation can you ignore?

a Calculate the relative formula masses of the relevant reactants and products.

relative atomic mass of Mg = ...   relative formula mass of H_2 = ...

b Calculate the masses of reactant and product, using the balanced equation.

1 Mg → 1 H_2, so 1 × 24 g Mg → 1 × .... g H_2

c Work out the mass for 1 g of reactant or product.

24 g Mg → .... g H_2 1 g Mg → $\dfrac{}{}$ g H_2

d Scale up to the mass given in the question. State your final answer.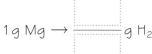

7.2 g Mg → ....

Chemistry

Sample response

To answer a question about calculations involving masses, you need to think about:
- the information given in the question that you need to use in your calculation
- explaining in words all of the steps involved
- showing all of your working out and including the units.

Consider this exam-style question.

Exam-style question

1 Calculate the mass of water produced when 3.2 g of methane, CH_4, completely burns in oxygen.

(relative atomic masses: H = 1, C = 12, O = 16)

$$CH_4(g) + 2O_2(g) \rightarrow CO_2(g) + 2H_2O(g)$$

The calculation below was written by a student, as a response to the exam-style question above.

M_r of CH_4 = 16, M_r of $2H_2O$ = 36
16 g of CH_4 makes 2 × 36 g of H_2O
1 g of CH_4 makes $\frac{72}{16}$ g of H_2O
3.2 g of CH_4 makes $\frac{72}{16}$ g × 3.2 of H_2O = 14.4

Think again about the steps to follow in calculations.
1 Identify the information you are given in the question.
2 Explain in words what you are calculating.
3 Substitute in the numbers you know and show your working out.
4 State the units of your answer.

1 Look again at the student response and check the answer.

a Identify ✎ two things the student has done well in the calculation.

Which steps have they included?

1 ....

2 ....

b Identify ✎ two things they need to do better next time.

Is the answer correct? Are the units correct?

1 ....

2 ....

Your turn!

It is now time to use what you have learned to answer the question below. Remember to read the question thoroughly, looking for clues. Make good use of your knowledge from other areas of chemistry.

Before you start to write your answers, think about the four steps to follow in a calculation. You can see these on page 94.

Exam-style question

1   A student wanted to make 24.0 g of the salt, sodium chloride.

(relative atomic masses: H = 1, C = 12, O = 16, Na = 23, Cl = 35.5)

The equation for the reaction is:

$Na_2CO_3(s) + 2HCl(aq) \rightarrow 2NaCl(aq) + H_2O(l) + CO_2(g)$

(a) The relative formula mass of sodium chloride is 58.5.

Calculate the relative formula mass of sodium carbonate, Na_2CO_3.

> Your calculation should include the relative atomic masses, multiplied by the number of each atom/ion in the chemical formula.

(1 mark)

(b) Calculate the mass of sodium carbonate the student should react with dilute hydrochloric acid to make 24.0 g of sodium chloride.

> This is a multi-step calculation, so include all of the steps.

(3 marks)

2   A sample of copper oxide was analysed and found to contain 1.27 g of copper and 0.32 g of oxygen.

Calculate the empirical formula of the copper oxide.

(relative atomic masses: O = 16, Cu = 63.5)

> **Remember** The empirical formula tells you the smallest whole number ratio of the atoms/ions of each element in the compound.

(3 marks)

Chemistry

Need more practice?

In the exam, questions about calculations involving using masses could occur as:

- simple standalone questions
- part of a question on another topic, for example, reactions of metals
- part of a question about a practical test.

Have a go at these exam-style questions.

Exam-style questions

1 Calculate the empirical formula of the compound formed when 15.9 g of copper reacts with 17.7 g of chlorine.

(relative atomic masses: $Cl = 35.5$, $Cu = 63.5$)

(3 marks)

2 The equation for the reaction between calcium oxide and dilute hydrochloric acid is:

$$CaO(s) + 2HCl(aq) \rightarrow CaCl_2(aq) + H_2O(l)$$

Calculate the mass of calcium chloride formed from 2.8 g of calcium oxide.

Give your answer to 2 significant figures.

> Calculation questions may ask you to give your answer to a specific number of significant figures. Look out for this.

(4 marks)

Boost your grade

To improve your grade further, practise different types of calculation involving masses. Follow the steps for calculations, including all working out, and remember to include the units.

How confident do you feel about each of these **skills?** Colour in the bars.

1 How do I set out calculations correctly?

2 How do I calculate empirical formulae?

3 How do I calculate the mass of a reactant or product?

⑥ Chemical formulae and equations

This unit will help you to write chemical formulae and equations for the reactions you study. In exam questions, you will be asked to complete, or write, word equations. You may be given a chemical equation to balance or you may be asked to write a fully balanced chemical equation.

In the exam, you will be asked to tackle questions such as the ones below.

Exam-style questions

1 When sodium hydroxide reacts with dilute sulfuric acid, the salt sodium sulfate and water are produced.

(a) Write a word equation for this reaction.

.... (2 marks)

(b) Balance the equation for the reaction of sodium hydroxide with sulfuric acid.

.... NaOH(aq) + H_2SO_4(aq) $\longrightarrow$ Na_2SO_4(aq) + ... H_2O(l)　　(2 marks)

2 Write the balanced equation for the reaction of sodium with water, to produce sodium hydroxide, NaOH, and hydrogen gas, H_2. Include state symbols.

.... (3 marks)

Chemistry

You will already have done some work on chemical formulae and equations. Before starting the **skills boosts**, rate your confidence in each area. Colour in 🖉 the bars.

> **1** How do I write chemical formulae?
>
> **2** How do I write word equations?
>
> **3** How do I write chemical equations?

Word equations and chemical equations show what happens in a chemical reaction.

In chemical equations, chemical formulae are used instead of words.

For example, carbon dioxide is a **covalent compound** formed when a non-metal reacts with a non-metal. It contains one carbon atom and two oxygen atoms, so the formula is CO_2. Every molecule of carbon dioxide has the same composition and the same chemical formula.

The word **formulae** is used when there is more than one **formula**.

The word **dioxide** gives a clue to the formula: 'di' = 2, 'oxide' refers to oxygen.

① **a** Write the chemical formula for carbon monoxide.

Do you know what 'mono' means?

....

b Chlorine is a non-metal in group 7. Two chlorine atoms are bonded together in a molecule. Write the chemical formula for chlorine.

....

c Natural gas contains methane. Methane is a covalent compound with the formula CH_4. Write the formula of a compound with two carbon atoms and six hydrogen atoms.

....

When a metal reacts with a non-metal, the end of the name of the non-metal in the compound changes to '-ide'. For example, sodium and chlorine react to form sodium chlor<u>ide</u>. Sodium chloride is an **ionic compound**.

② Predict the name of the compound formed when:

a zinc reacts with oxygen

....

Skills boost 1 shows you how to write chemical formulae for ionic compounds.

b potassium reacts with bromine

....

Ball and stick models can be used to show atoms of elements and compounds.

③ Write the chemical formula of this compound.

The black spheres show carbon atoms and the white spheres show hydrogen atoms.

Count the number of atoms.

....

How do I write chemical formulae?

A chemical formula shows the atoms in an element or compound.
You may be asked to say how many of each atom are represented in a chemical formula.

When a metal reacts with a non-metal, an ionic compound is formed.

The table below shows you how to work out the chemical formula of an ionic compound such as magnesium chloride.

	Step	Example
1	Write down the symbols for the metal and the non-metal.	Mg and Cl
2	Use your periodic table to work out the charges on the ions.	Mg^{2+} and Cl^-
3	Balance the charges: $2 \times Cl^-$ ions are needed to balance the 2+ charge on Mg^{2+}.	$(+2) + (-1) + (-1) = 0$
4	Write down the chemical formula, using subscripts to show the number of atoms or ions.	$MgCl_2$

Magnesium is in group 2, so it loses 2 electrons to form a 2+ ion. Chlorine is in group 7, so it gains one electron to form a 1− ion.

To balance, the charges need to add up to zero.

There is no need to show the subscript for Mg because it is 1.

(1) Follow the steps below to write 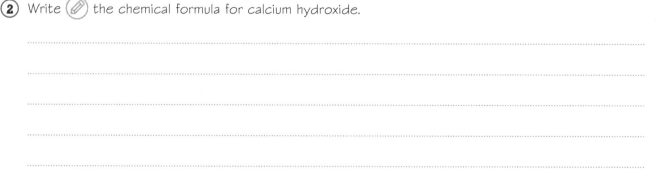 the chemical formula for sodium oxide.

   (a) Write down the symbols for the metal and the non-metal.

   ....

   (b) Use your periodic table to work out the charges on the ions.

   ....

   (c) Balance the charges.

   ....

   (d) Write down the chemical formula, using subscripts to show the number of atoms or ions.

   ....

Some ions are **polyatomic**. This means they contain more than one atom, e.g. the hydroxide ion is OH^-.

When a chemical formula has two or more polyatomic ions, the formula of the ion is written in a bracket.

For example, magnesium hydroxide is $Mg(OH)_2$.

The '2' outside the brackets means there is two times everything inside the brackets.

(2) Write the chemical formula for calcium hydroxide.

....

....

....

....

Chemistry

2 How do I write word equations?

Word equations can be used to show what happens when chemical reactions take place. They show the **reactants** (the substances that react together) and the **products** (the substances that are made) in a reaction.

In a word equation, the arrow (⟶) means 'gives', so it shows you what products are formed.

When magnesium burns in oxygen, magnesium oxide is formed. The word equation for the reaction is:

magnesium + oxygen ⟶ magnesium oxide

(1) Look at the word equation above.

  (a) Underline (A) the reactants.

  (b) How many products are formed in this reaction? Circle (A) the correct answer.

  | 1 | 2 | 3 | 4 |

  Look at the word equation to see how many substances are produced.

  (c) Explain your answer to (b).

  ....

  ....

The general reaction for an acid reacting with a base (a metal oxide, a metal hydroxide or a metal carbonate) is:

acid + base ⟶ salt + water

(2) The salt zinc sulfate can be made by reacting zinc oxide with dilute sulfuric acid.

Write (✎) a word equation for this reaction.

The word **dilute** does not need to be included in the word equation.

....

(3) (a) What is the name of the salt produced in the reaction between sodium hydroxide and dilute hydrochloric acid?

Look back at pages 66–67 to remind yourself of the rules for naming salts.

Tick (✓) the correct answer.

sodium sulfate ☐

sodium nitrate ☐

sodium chloride ☐

sodium phosphate ☐

  (b) Write (✎) a word equation for the reaction between sodium hydroxide and dilute hydrochloric acid.

....

3 How do I write chemical equations?

You will be asked to write **balanced chemical equations**. These equations include the chemical formulae of the reactants and the products.

Balanced chemical equations show the reactants at the start and the products formed at the end of a reaction. For example, when magnesium burns in oxygen, magnesium oxide is formed:

$$\text{magnesium} + \text{oxygen} \longrightarrow \text{magnesium oxide}$$

If we simply replace the words in the word equation with chemical formulae, we get:

$Mg(s) + O_2(g) \longrightarrow MgO(s)$ State symbols are included in chemical equations: (s) = solid, (l) = liquid, (g) = gas and (aq) = aqueous solution. Dilute acids are (aq).

This equation is not balanced. There should be the same number of atoms of each element at the start and at the end of the reaction.

To balance the equation:

1   count how many atoms of each element there are

2   write a big number in front of a chemical formula if it is not balanced (e.g. **2**MgO)

3   note that the big numbers multiply all of the atoms in the formula

4   count again, to check that the number of atoms of each element is the same on both sides of the equation.

You may need to work through this list a couple of times until the equation is balanced.

In the $Mg + O_2$ example above, there are two atoms of oxygen in O_2. In the product, each oxygen atom bonds to one magnesium atom. This means there must be two magnesium atoms to react with the two oxygen atoms in O_2.

Write 2 in front of the MgO to balance the O atoms.

Now you have 2 Mg atoms, so write 2 in front of the Mg on the left-hand side of the equation to balance the Mg atoms.

The balanced equation is:

$\textbf{2}Mg(s) + O_2(g) \longrightarrow \textbf{2}MgO(s)$

(1) Balance the equation for the reaction of zinc with oxygen to form zinc oxide. ✎

.... $Zn(s) + O_2(g) \longrightarrow$ .... $ZnO(s)$

(2) Balance the equation for the reaction between potassium and water, to form potassium hydroxide and hydrogen. ✎

.... $K(s) +$ .... $H_2O(l) \longrightarrow$ .... $KOH(aq) + H_2(g)$

You may find it helpful to count the number of atoms of each element on each side of the equation.

	Number of atoms on reactants side		Number of atoms on products side	
	Original equation	Balanced equation	Original equation	Balanced equation
potassium, K				
oxygen, O				
hydrogen, H				

Chemistry

Sample response

When you write chemical formulae and equations, you need to check that:
- all the reactants and products are included in the equation
- the symbols are written correctly
- the chemical equation is balanced.

Look at the exam-style question and sample student answer below.

Exam-style question

1 The salt sodium chloride is formed when solid sodium carbonate, Na_2CO_3, reacts with dilute hydrochloric acid. Water and carbon dioxide are also formed.

(a) Write the word equation for the reaction.

.... (1 mark)

(b) Write the balanced chemical equation for the reaction, including state symbols.

.... (3 marks)

The answer below was written by a student.

---

1 (a) sodium carbonate + dilute hydrochloric acid → sodium chloride salt + water + carbon dioxide

(b) $2Na_2CO_3(s) + 2HCl(aq) \rightarrow 2NaCl(aq) + 2H_2O(l) + 3Co_2(g)$

---

(1) The student's word equation is almost correct. Write 🖊 two changes you would make to the word equation.

....

....

(2) Is the student's chemical equation correct, in terms of formulae and balancing? You can use your periodic table to check chemical formulae.

$$2Na_2CO_3(s) + 2HCl(aq) \rightarrow 2NaCl(aq) + H_2O(l) + 3Co_2(g)$$

a Tick ✓ where the chemical formulae and balancing are correct.

b Make 🖊 any corrections in the table below.

Formula	Correct? ✓ / ✗	Correction
Reactants: Na_2CO_3 + HCl		
Products: $NaCl + H_2O + Co_2$		
Balancing: $2Na_2CO_3 + 2HCl \rightarrow 2NaCl + H_2O + 3Co_2$		

c Write 🖊 the correct balanced equation.

....

Your turn!

It is now time to use what you have learned to answer the question below. Remember to read the question thoroughly, looking for clues. Make good use of your knowledge from other areas of chemistry.

Read through the exam-style question and answer it using the guided steps below.

Exam-style questions

1   When sodium hydroxide reacts with dilute sulfuric acid, the salt sodium sulfate and water are produced.

   (a) Write a word equation for this reaction.

   .... (2 marks)

   (b) Balance the equation for the reaction of sodium hydroxide with sulfuric acid.

       .... $NaOH(aq)$ + $H_2SO_4(aq)$ → $Na_2SO_4(aq)$ + ... $H_2O(l)$ (2 marks)

2   Write the balanced equation for the reaction of sodium with water, to produce sodium hydroxide, NaOH, and hydrogen gas, H_2. Include state symbols.

   .... (3 marks)

---

1   a   Write 🖉 the word equation.   Reactants are on the left of the arrow, products are on the right of the arrow.

. . . .

   b   Balance the chemical equation. Use the table below to help you. 🖉

       .... $NaOH(aq)$ + $H_2SO_4(aq)$ → $Na_2SO_4(aq)$ + ... $H_2O(l)$

                        Count the number of atoms of each element on each side of the equation.

	Number of atoms on reactants side		Number of atoms on products side	
	Original equation	Balanced equation	Original equation	Balanced equation
sodium, Na				
oxygen, O				
hydrogen, H				
sulfur, S				

                        Remember hydrogen is a diatomic molecule (H_2).

2   Write 🖉 the balanced chemical equation for question 2.

. . . .

                                    Check all formulae are correct and make sure the equation is balanced.

Chemistry

Need more practice?

Exam questions about chemical formulae and equations could occur as:

- simple standalone questions
- part of a question on, for example, reactions of acids
- part of a question about a practical test.

Have a go at this exam-style question.

Exam-style question

1   To test for carbon dioxide, the gas is bubbled through limewater. Limewater is calcium hydroxide solution, $Ca(OH)_2$. If the limewater turns cloudy, the gas is carbon dioxide. The limewater turns cloudy because an insoluble precipitate of calcium carbonate is produced. The other product from this reaction formed is water, H_2O.

(a) Give the state symbol that would be used for calcium carbonate in the chemical equation.

....

(1 mark)

(b) Write the word equation for the reaction.

....

....

(1 mark)

(c) Write the balanced chemical equation for the reaction.

....

....

(3 marks)

Boost your grade

To improve your grade, practise writing word equations and chemical equations for all the chemical reactions you learn about.

How confident do you feel about each of these **skills?** Colour in the bars.

1 **How do I write chemical formulae?**

2 **How do I write word equations?**

3 **How do I write chemical equations?**

⑦ Answering extended response questions

This unit will help you to answer extended open response questions by deciding what is being asked, and then planning a concise answer with the right amount of detail.

In the exam, you will be asked to tackle questions such as the one below.

1   The alkali metals in group 1 of the periodic table include lithium, sodium and potassium.

   The alkali metals show a pattern in their reactivity with water.

   This pattern can be seen when lithium, sodium and potassium are added separately to water.

   Explain, using examples from the reactions with water, the pattern in reactivity of the group 1 metals.

   You may include equations as part of your answer.

   ....   (6 marks)

You will already have done some work on extended response questions. Before starting the **skills boosts**, rate your confidence in answering this type of question. Colour in the bars.

① **How do I know what the question is asking me to do?**

② **How do I plan my answer?**

③ **How do I choose the right detail to answer the question concisely?**

Chemistry

The marks given for extended response questions depend on:
- the level of understanding shown in the detail of what you have written
- how well your answer is organised.

(1) Think about how you usually answer extended response questions.

Write ✎ any ideas you have tried out that would help other students.

Your teacher may have given you some top tips. Can you say which method has been the most successful?

....

....

....

(2) Have you tried any of these methods when answering extended response questions?

Circle (A) **Yes** or **No**.

a	Underlining/highlighting and then thinking about the **command word**.	Yes / No
b	Highlighting any **key information** given in the question, e.g. from a table of information or a graph.	Yes / No
c	Thinking about **scientific ideas** to include in your answer.	Yes / No
d	Thinking about what type of conjunction to use, e.g. 'and' or 'because'.	Yes / No
e	**Checking** to see if you have answered the question that has been asked.	Yes / No
f	Writing a rough **outline** of your answer before writing the final version.	Yes / No

(3) Which **two** ideas from the list above do you think would help you to answer extended response questions better? ✎

1 ....

2 ....

(4) Explain ✎ why you think these ideas would help you to answer extended response questions.

....

....

....

....

....

How do I know what the question is asking me to do?

The **command word** given in a question is the starting point to help you to decide how to answer the question. The question may also contain information that will guide you to the correct answer.

Read this exam-style question.

Exam-style question

1   The table below shows information about fractions obtained from crude oil.

Fraction	Number of carbon atoms in molecules	Percentage obtained from crude oil	Percentage required by customers
Petrol	5 to 10	10	26
Kerosene	10 to 16	13	8

Explain why it is necessary for oil companies to use cracking on some fractions obtained from crude oil.

Include ideas about the cracking process in your answer.

.... (6 marks)

① Identify the useful information given in the question text.

a Highlight 🖉 the **command word**.

What does this tell you? 🖉 ....

b Circle Ⓐ the name of the **process** or **reaction** the question is about.

What do you know about this? 🖉 ....

....

c Underline Ⓐ the text that describes what the **main part** of your answer should focus on.

d Highlight 🖉 the relevant **data** or **information** that you should use to help you to answer the question.

The question gives data for petrol and for kerosene.

What does this tell you? 🖉 ....

e Annotate 🖉 the question with any **extra clues**.

What does this tell you? 🖉 ....

....

② Using your answers to ①, summarise 🖉 what you think the question is asking you to do.

....

....

....

....

② How do I plan my answer?

You can plan your answer by:
- deciding how to use any information or data given in the question, to support your answer
- thinking about the topic to identify relevant points.

Read the following exam-style question.

Exam-style question

1 At room temperature, hydrogen peroxide solution decomposes slowly to form water and oxygen gas. The equation for the reaction is:

$$hydrogen\ peroxide \rightarrow water + oxygen$$

The progress of the reaction can be followed by measuring the volume of gas given off.

This reaction can be catalysed by the addition of solid manganese(IV) oxide.

Two properties of a catalyst are:
- it increases the rate of a reaction
- its mass is unchanged at the end of the reaction.

Describe experiments to show that manganese(IV) oxide has these properties when used as a catalyst in this reaction.

.... (6 marks)

① Highlight ✎ the **command** word.

Describe means 'Give an account of something, or link facts, information, events or processes in a logical order'.

② **Identify** useful information given in the question by circling Ⓐ, underlining A and annotating ✎.

③ **Organise** your ideas by thinking about the information given and what this tells you.

Write ✎ a plan on paper.

For a practical question, think about the variables involved, the apparatus and chemicals to be used and the order of the method steps to be carried out.

Now start to build up the material you need to answer the question.

Write ✎ your answers to the following questions on a separate sheet of paper.

④ 'The progress of the reaction can be followed by measuring the volume of gas given off.'

What is the gas produced and how can you measure the volume of gas given off?

⑤ 'This reaction can be catalysed by the addition of solid manganese(IV) oxide.'

The question tells you about the two properties of catalysts you need to discuss.

  a How can you show that the catalyst increases the rate of reaction?

  What variables will you control and measure?

  b How can you show the mass is unchanged?

  What apparatus will you use to measure the amounts of chemicals and the rate of the reaction?

3 How do I choose the right detail to answer the question concisely?

To answer a question concisely, using the correct details:
- think through what you know about the topic and choose the relevant scientific knowledge and/or practical experience to answer the question
- order your ideas in a logical way, clearly linking them together to answer the question.

Look at your planning ideas for the extended response question on page 108. Now you need to decide what is relevant and what is not.

(1) Look at the **command** word again. Read the three scientific ideas about a catalyst below and tick ✓ those that are relevant to answering the question. You can tick more than one box.

Is the question asking you to explain why the manganese(IV) oxide acts as a catalyst?

A Catalysts speed up chemical reactions without being permanently changed.

B A catalyst lowers the activation energy for a reaction, so more reactant molecules have enough energy and more collisions are successful.

C The hydrogen peroxide will decompose faster when the catalyst is added.

(2) If manganese(IV) oxide acts as a catalyst for this reaction, what results would you expect? Tick ✓ the correct boxes. You can tick more than one box.

Think about how a catalyst will affect the results of the experiment.

A The experiment with the catalyst added will give off the same volume of gas, but in a shorter time.

B The mass of manganese(IV) oxide will be less at the end of the experiment than at the start.

C A catalyst is not used up, so if 1 g of catalyst is added at the start, then 1 g will be recovered at the end.

Decide how you will order your points. To order your points in a logical way, think about:

- the variables to be considered
- the clear and logical method steps
- the apparatus you would use to measure the chemicals and the rate of reaction
- the expected results of the experiments.

Will the experiment work?

(3) Now outline your answer here ✏ using the material from this page and page 108. Look back at page 108 to remind yourself of the question.

You may need to complete your answer on another piece of paper.

....
....
....
....
....
....

Chemistry

Sample response

To answer an extended response question, you need to think about:
- what the question is about
- how to plan your answer to include all of the information required.

Exam-style question

1 The table below shows information about fractions obtained from crude oil.

Fraction	Number of carbon atoms in molecules	Percentage obtained from crude oil	Percentage required by customers
Petrol	5 to 10	10	26
Kerosene	10 to 16	13	8

Explain why it is necessary for oil companies to use cracking on some fractions obtained from crude oil.

Include ideas about the cracking process in your answer.

.... (6 marks)

The answer below was written by a student.

> Oil companies use cracking so they can meet the demands of customers for the amount of petrol required and they do not have too much kerosene left over. Cracking is a process which breaks down larger hydrocarbon molecules into smaller, more useful ones. The smaller molecules are more useful, as fuels, e.g. petrol.
> Kerosene is a fraction containing larger molecules, as there are more carbon atoms. Some kerosene can be broken down by cracking to produce petrol.

(1) Which parts of the answer are well written?

a Highlight ✎ where the student has included ideas about the cracking process.

b Underline Ⓐ where the student has explained why oil companies use cracking.

(2) Where does the student need to improve?

a Has the student used any of the data/information provided to support their explanation?

Circle Ⓐ the answer. **Yes / No**

b Explain ✎ your answer to a and include any additional information that would improve the student answer.

....

....

....

....

....

....

Your turn!

It is now time to use what you have learned to answer the question below. Remember to read the question thoroughly, looking for clues. Make good use of your knowledge from other areas of chemistry.

Exam-style question

1 The alkali metals in group 1 of the periodic table include lithium, sodium and potassium.

The alkali metals show a pattern in their reactivity with water.

This pattern can be seen when lithium, sodium and potassium are added separately to water.

Explain, using examples from the reactions with water, the pattern in reactivity of the group 1 metals.

You may include equations as part of your answer.

.... (6 marks)

Use this checklist when writing your answer.

Checklist	✓
Command word: highlight the command word and think about what it is asking you to do.	
Identify useful **information** given in the question. Use highlighting, circles, underlining, ticks and shading.	
Organise your ideas by thinking about the information given and what this tells you.	
Decide what to include from your own knowledge and understanding of the topic.	

(1) Plan ✐ an outline of your answer below. Use these prompts to help.

Group 1 metals: What is the order of reactivity?

....

Reactions: What would you see? What products are formed?

....

Equation: Write a balanced equation for one of the reactions, including state symbols.

....

Trends: How do the reactions change from lithium to potassium? What is the same?
What is different?

....

....

Why does the reactivity change? Use ideas about electronic configuration. Think about how easily the outer shell electron is lost.

....

....

(2) Now write ✐ your answer on a separate piece of paper.

Need more practice?

In the exam, extended answer questions could occur as:

- simple standalone questions
- part of a question about any topic you have studied, e.g. bonding and structure or fuels
- part of a question about a practical test.

Have a go at these exam-style questions. 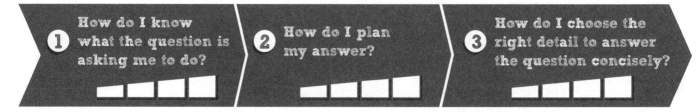 You may need to continue on a separate piece of paper.

Exam-style questions

1 The halogens chlorine, bromine and iodine are in group 7 of the periodic table.

Explain the trend in reactivity of the halogens.

....

....

....

....

(6 marks)

2 Describe the experimental procedure to carry out a titration to find the exact volume of hydrochloric acid needed to neutralise 25.0 cm³ of sodium hydroxide solution and obtain pure, dry crystals of sodium chloride.

....

....

....

....

....

(6 marks)

Boost your grade

To improve your grade in extended response questions, practise:

o using the prompts in this unit to help you to think about what the question is asking

o planning your answers to extended response questions before writing the final version.

How confident do you feel about each of these **skills?** Colour in ✐ the bars.

1 How do I know what the question is asking me to do?

2 How do I plan my answer?

3 How do I choose the right detail to answer the question concisely?

① Energy transfers

This unit will help you to learn more about energy transfers, including wasted energy and efficiency.

In the exam, you will be asked to tackle questions such as the one below.

1 Figure 1 shows a battery-operated vacuum cleaner being used.

Figure 1

(a) Describe the useful energy transfer taking place in the vacuum cleaner.

....   (1 mark)

(b) (i) Identify **one** way energy is wasted in the vacuum cleaner.

....   (1 mark)

(ii) Describe what happens to this wasted energy.

....   (1 mark)

(c) For every 100 J of energy transferred by the vacuum cleaner, 35 J is usefully transferred.

Calculate the efficiency of the vacuum cleaner.

....   (3 marks)

You will already have done some work on energy transfers. Before starting the **skills boosts**, rate your confidence in each area. Colour in 🖉 the bars.

① How can I correctly identify energy transfers in a range of contexts?

② How can I explain what happens to wasted energy?

③ How do I answer questions about efficiency?

Physics

Energy is something that is needed to make things happen or change. It is measured in joules (J).
Energy cannot be created or destroyed but it can be stored and transferred between stores.

1 Draw lines to match each energy store to where the energy is stored. One has been done for you.

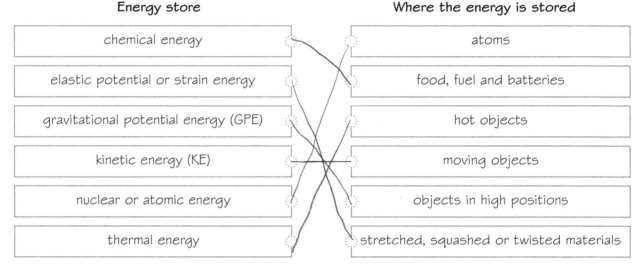

Energy store	Where the energy is stored
chemical energy	atoms
elastic potential or strain energy	food, fuel and batteries
gravitational potential energy (GPE)	hot objects
kinetic energy (KE)	moving objects
nuclear or atomic energy	objects in high positions
thermal energy	stretched, squashed or twisted materials

Energy can be transferred between different stores by:

- electricity – from a power station, generator or objects run on batteries
- forces – tension in a spring, friction between moving surfaces, impacts
- heat – from hot substances
- light – from light sources
- sound – from sound sources.

2 a State how energy is transferred:

i to bicycle brake pads ....

ii to an electric heater ....

iii from an electric heater ....

b Circle the correct words to complete this student's response.

A battery-operated radio gets warm as it plays music. Energy is transferred by
forces / sound / electricity to the radio. Then energy is transferred by the radio
as **chemical / sound** and also by heating to transfer **thermal / kinetic** energy to
the radio and the surroundings.

Energy stores and transfers can be shown in diagrams. **Sankey diagrams**
show the **amount** of energy transferred.

Here is a Sankey diagram for making toast.

100 J energy
transferred to
the toaster by
electricity

80 J energy transferred
by heat to heat the
bread in the toaster
(useful energy transfer)

20 J energy transferred by heat to heat
the toaster and the surrounding air and
surface (wasted energy transfer)

1 How can I correctly identify energy transfers in a range of contexts?

To be able to identify energy transfers, you need to learn and recognise the different energy stores.

1 Circle Ⓐ the correct sentence in each column to show the energy transfers in a battery-operated whisk. The energy transfers during photosynthesis are shown as an example.

	How is energy stored at the start?	How is energy transferred? (electricity, forces, heat, light, or sound)	How is energy stored at the end?
Photosynthesis	energy stored in the Sun as nuclear energy	energy transferred by light	energy stored in plants as chemical energy
Battery-operated whisk	energy stored as kinetic energy	energy stored as kinetic energy	energy stored as kinetic energy
	energy stored in the battery as chemical energy	energy stored in the battery as chemical energy	energy stored in the battery as chemical energy
	energy transferred by electricity	energy transferred by electricity	energy transferred by electricity

The battery provides electricity which turns a motor to **spin** the whisk.

2 Complete the table by writing ✎ the energy transfers for a toy car and a twig falling from a tree.

	How is energy stored at the start?	How is energy transferred?	How is energy stored at the end?
a A toy car that moves when a spring is released **What makes the toy car move?**			
b A twig falling from a tree **How is energy stored in objects above the ground?**			

2 How can I explain what happens to wasted energy?

You need to think about where energy is stored after it has been transferred, and whether this is a useful store or not. Energy is often spread out into the surroundings as heat.

1 **a** For both an electric toothbrush and a hairdryer, energy is transferred by electricity to an energy store. Circle Ⓐ the **three** energy stores.

| chemical | gravitational potential | kinetic | sound | thermal |

b Complete 🖉 the table using the three energy stores you identified in **1** **a** to show whether these energy transfers are useful or wasted for each device.

An energy transfer is **wasted** if we do not make use of the energy transferred.

	Useful energy store	Wasted energy store
electric toothbrush		
electric hairdryer		

2 A tile on a roof stores energy as gravitational potential energy (GPE) because it is above the ground. It falls off the roof and breaks into pieces when it hits the ground.

Remember The total amount of energy in a system always remains the same.

a Complete 🖉 the sentences using words from the box – you can use them more than once if needed.

The **bold** words will help you with the answers.

| chemical | GPE | kinetic | strain |

i As the tile **falls**, GPE is transferred to .... energy.

ii As the tile breaks, the pieces bounce **up** and around so they have ....

and .... energy.

b Where is the energy when the pieces lie on the ground and have stopped moving? 🖉

The tile is on the ground so does it have GPE? It is not moving so does it have kinetic energy?

....

c Energy is always stored or transferred. Tick ✓ **one** box.

The energy:

i is still stored as GPE in the tile. ☐

ii has been dissipated (spread out) to the ground and the surrounding air as heat. ☐

iii has been destroyed. ☐

iv is stored as GPE in the ground. ☐

3 How do I answer questions about efficiency?

Efficiency is about how much input energy is transferred to a useful form, and how much is wasted.

There are three steps to an efficiency calculation.

1 Write down the equation you will use to calculate efficiency:

$$\text{efficiency} = \frac{\text{useful energy transferred by the device}}{\text{total energy supplied to the device}}$$

2 Find and substitute the correct values from the question.

3 Calculate the answer.

> **Efficiency** is the proportion of input energy that is transferred to a useful form. A more efficient machine wastes less energy.

> Learn this equation! You need to be able to recall and use it.

① A car has an input energy of 200 J of chemical energy from fuel. 50 J of energy is transferred to useful kinetic energy and 150 J is wasted as heat. Calculate the efficiency of the car.

a Write 🖉 the equation you will use to calculate efficiency.

b Find this information in the question:

   i Highlight 🖉 the device.

   ii Circle Ⓐ how much energy is supplied to the car engine.

   iii Underline Ⓐ how much of this energy is transferred as useful energy.

c Substitute 🖉 these values into the equation and calculate the answer.

Efficiency of car = ...

> Your answer should be a decimal between 0 and 1.

> In an exam, you would get 3 marks just for writing the correct answer. However, if you got the answer wrong, you could still get marks for showing correct working.

Efficiency is a ratio or proportion so it **does not need a unit**.

It is sometimes converted to a percentage by multiplying by 100.

For example: Efficiency = 0.35 <u>or</u> 0.35 × 100 = 35%

Sample response

Here are some exam-style questions. Use the student responses to these questions to improve your understanding.

Exam-style question

Describe the energy transfers when a ball is thrown up into the air and falls back down again.

A
> Kinetic and potential energy.

B
> As the ball moves up, kinetic energy is transferred to gravitational potential energy. As the ball falls back down, the gravitational potential energy is transferred to kinetic energy.

(1) Give ✏ two reasons why answer **B** is better than answer **A**.

a ....

b ....

Exam-style question

Explain what happens to the energy transferred by electricity when a kettle boils water.

An answer to an **explain** question needs a reason.

C
> It is transferred as heat and some is lost.

D
> The energy is transferred to thermal energy which is used to heat up the water and some is lost to the surroundings.

(2) Does answer **C** 'describe' or 'explain' what happens to the energy? ✏ ....

(3) Answer **D** gets 3 marks. Circle Ⓐ the parts of the answer where you think the marks are given.

Exam-style question

Calculate the efficiency of this motor.

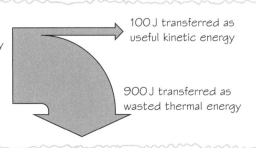

1000 J of energy transferred by electricity to the motor

100 J transferred as useful kinetic energy

900 J transferred as wasted thermal energy

(4) Student E gave an answer of ....9.... and showed no working so they would gain 0 marks.

Answer ✏ these questions to work out the correct answer.

a What is the value for the useful energy transferred by the device? ....

b What is the value for the total energy supplied to the device? ....

c How do you know this answer is not correct, without doing any calculation? ....

....

d What is the correct answer? ....

Your turn!

It is now time to use what you have learned to answer this question. Remember to read the question thoroughly, looking for clues. Make good use of your knowledge from other areas of physics.

Exam-style question

1   Figure 1 shows a battery-operated vacuum cleaner being used.

Figure 1

(a) Describe the useful energy transfer taking place in the vacuum cleaner.   **(1 mark)**

(b) (i)   Identify **one** way energy is wasted in the vacuum cleaner.   **(1 mark)**

      (ii) Describe what happens to this wasted energy.   **(1 mark)**

(c) For every 100 J of energy transferred by the vacuum cleaner, 35 J is usefully transferred.

      Calculate the efficiency of the vacuum cleaner.   **(3 marks)**

① Work through and give 🖉 your answers to the exam-style question here.

> Where is the energy stored at the start? What does a vacuum cleaner do?

(a) ....

(b) (i) ....

      (ii) ....

(c) Write 🖉 the equation for efficiency.

Efficiency =

Now complete the calculation and write 🖉 the answer.

Efficiency =

> What is the useful energy transferred by the device?
>
> What is the total energy supplied to the device?

Physics

Need more practice?

In the exam, questions about energy transfer could occur as:

- simple standalone questions
- part of a question on energy, electricity or forces
- part of a question about a practical test.

Have a go at these exam-style questions.

Exam-style questions

1 (a) Describe a useful energy transfer in a television.

.... (1 mark)

   (b) Explain an energy transfer in the television that is not useful.

....

....

.... (2 marks)

2 A petrol lawnmower has an efficiency of 0.2.

   Calculate how much energy is transferred as useful kinetic energy when 50 J is supplied.

.... (4 marks)

Boost your grade

For more challenging 4-mark efficiency calculations, there is usually an extra fourth step. For example, you may be given the value for wasted energy and asked to work out the value for useful energy.

How confident do you feel about each of these **skills?** Colour in the bars.

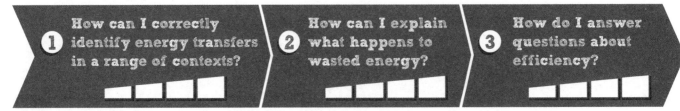

1 How can I correctly identify energy transfers in a range of contexts?

2 How can I explain what happens to wasted energy?

3 How do I answer questions about efficiency?

② Forces and motion

This unit will help you to learn more about resultant forces, and how to describe and interpret distance/time and velocity/time graphs.

In the exam, you will be asked to tackle questions such as the one below.

Exam-style question

1 A Segway rider moves forward in a straight line at a constant speed.

(a) Which row of the table shows the correct description of the forces on the Segway?

		vertical direction	horizontal direction
☒	A	balanced forces	balanced forces
☒	B	unbalanced forces	balanced forces
☒	C	balanced forces	unbalanced forces
☒	D	unbalanced forces	unbalanced forces

(1 mark)

(b) The rider slows down as she goes uphill.

Explain the effect this has on the resultant force on the Segway.

.... (2 marks)

(c) Figure 1 shows a distance/time graph of a 5-minute Segway ride.

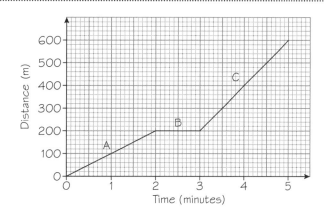

Figure 1

(i) Describe and compare the three stages of the journey, A, B and C.

.... (3 marks)

(ii) Calculate the speed of the Segway in m/s for part A.

speed = ... m/s (4 marks)

You will already have done some work on forces and motion. Before starting the **skills boosts**, rate your confidence in each area. Colour in the bars.

1 **How do I describe the effects of a resultant force?**

2 **How do I describe distance/time graphs?**

3 **How do I interpret velocity/time graphs?**

A force is a pull, push or twist and is measured in newtons (N). A force is needed to make an object start moving, keep moving, change speed, or stop. Force is a vector quantity. This means it has both magnitude (size) and direction.

1. The box shows four forces – A, B, C and D – acting on an object. An arrow is used to show the **size** and **direction** of each force.

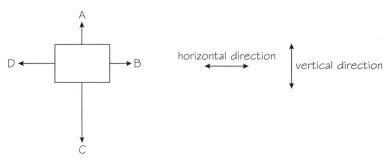

Answer ✐ the following questions about the diagram.

a i Which is the largest force? ....

  ii How do you know? ....

b i Which pair of forces is in the horizontal direction? .... and ....

  ii Which pair of forces is in the vertical direction? .... and ....

When two or more forces act on an object, they can be combined into a single force called the **resultant force**.

To calculate the resultant of two forces that are in line:

- add them if they are in the same direction
- find the difference if they are in opposite directions.

2. Force B is 3 N and force D is 5 N. The forces are acting in opposite directions. Calculate the resultant force in the horizontal direction. ✐

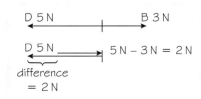

> The resultant force in the horizontal direction is .... to the left.

3. Force A is 3 N and force C is 8 N. Calculate the resultant force in the vertical direction. ✐

Do you need to add the forces or find the difference between them?

> The resultant force in the vertical direction is ....

Remember both size and direction.

4. Tick ✓ the equation used to calculate speed.

| $speed = \dfrac{distance}{time}$ | ☐ |

| $speed = distance \times time$ | ☐ |

| $speed = \dfrac{time}{distance}$ | ☐ |

1 How do I describe the effects of a resultant force?

To describe the effects of a resultant force on an object, you need to know two things about the force: the magnitude (size) and the direction. You can then describe how the force will affect the movement of an object.

When the forces acting on an object are **balanced**, there is no resultant force. This means that the speed and direction of the object will not change. If the object is stationary, it will stay stationary. If the object is moving, it will continue to move at a constant speed in the same direction

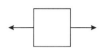

When the forces acting on an object are **unbalanced**, there is a resultant force. This means that the speed and/or direction of the object will change.

When the velocity changes, an object **accelerates**.

Remember Velocity is speed and direction, so the velocity changes.

1 The diagram on the right shows two forces acting on an object.
Circle Ⓐ the correct words in the table below.

	Answer 1	Answer 2
i The forces are	balanced	unbalanced
ii There is a resultant force	to the left	to the right
iii The velocity of the object	stays the same	changes
iv The object	accelerates	does not accelerate

2 The diagram shows the forces acting on a moped that is being driven along a road.

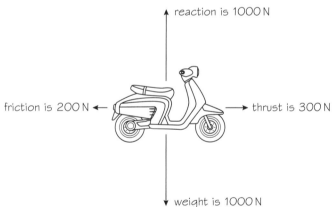

reaction is 1000 N

friction is 200 N ←　　　→ thrust is 300 N

weight is 1000 N

a Write ✐ which forces are balanced. .... and ....

b i Is there a resultant force in the vertical direction? Circle Ⓐ the answer. **Yes / No**

ii Write ✐ what effect this has on movement in the vertical direction.

....

c Complete ✐ these sentences.

In the horizontal direction, the forces are unbalanced. There is a resultant force of

100 N to the .... The velocity of the object ....

so the moped accelerates forwards.

Physics

2 How do I describe distance/time graphs?

A **distance/time graph** gives us information about the journey of an object. To describe or draw a distance/time graph, you need to understand how the object is moving. The speed of the object can also be found from the graph.

This is a distance/time graph of a moving object.

A–B: The object travels 5 m in 5 s.

B–C: The object stays 5 m away from the start for 3 s. It is not moving.

C–D: The object moves 5 m back to the starting point in 2 s.

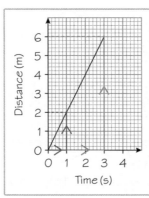

A–B: Constant speed away from start   B–C: Stationary

C–D: Constant speed back to the start point

On a distance/time graph, the gradient represents the speed of the journey. You can calculate the speed by finding the gradient, as shown on the right.

Move across 1 s; graph line goes up 2 m, so 2 m in 1 s:

$$\text{speed} = \frac{\text{distance}}{\text{time}} = \frac{2\,m}{1\,s} = 2\,m/s$$

or

The object has travelled 6 m in 3 s.

$$\text{speed} = \frac{\text{distance}}{\text{time}} = \frac{6\,m}{3\,s} = 2\,m/s$$

① Now look at this distance/time graph.

   a Calculate 🖉 the speed of the object for journey B.

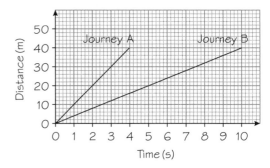

   b The line for journey A is steeper than the line for journey B.
Write 🖉 what this tells you about the speed.

....

   c Calculate 🖉 the speed of the object for journey A.

3 How do I interpret velocity/time graphs?

A **velocity/time** graph gives us information about the journey of an object. To interpret a velocity/time graph, you need to understand how the object is moving. You can also work out the acceleration of the object and the distance travelled during the journey.

This is a velocity/time graph of a moving object.

A–B: The object speeds up from 0 m/s to 5 m/s in 5 s.

B–C: The time between B and C is 2 s.

C–D: The object slows down from 5 m/s to 0 m/s in 1 s.

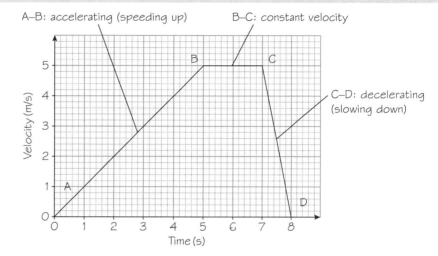

A–B: accelerating (speeding up) B–C: constant velocity

C–D: decelerating (slowing down)

The acceleration of the object can be calculated from the gradient of the slope (see page 124). The distance travelled can be found by calculating the area under that part of the graph, as shown below.

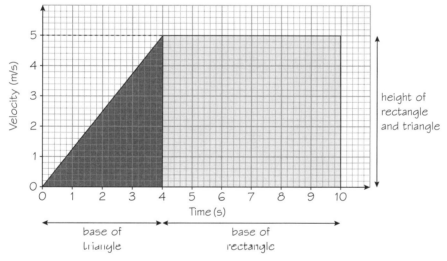

base of triangle

base of rectangle

distance travelled in the first 4 seconds = area of a triangle

$$= \frac{1}{2} \times \text{base of triangle} \times \text{height of triangle}$$

$$= \frac{1}{2} \times 4\,s \times 5\,m/s$$

$$= 10\,m$$

(1) Calculate the distance travelled between 4 and 10 seconds. 🖉

The area of a rectangle = base × height. The base is the difference in time between 4 and 10, i.e. 10 − 4 = 6 s. Remember the units.

distance travelled = ... × .... = ...

(2) Write 🖉 the total distance travelled over the 10 s.

total distance = ... + ... = ...

Sample response

Use these example student responses to improve your understanding. Look carefully to see what sort of graph you are being asked to describe and the information you can get from it.

1 (a) Describe the journey of the object shown by this velocity/time graph for parts A, B, C and D.

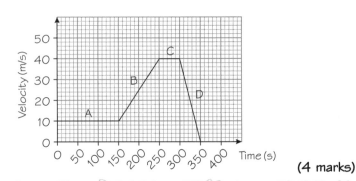

(4 marks)

① **a** Look at this student response. Then use the hints and highlights to write ✐ an improved answer for each section.

> A: The object is stationary for 150 seconds.
> B: It then moves at a constant speed for 250 seconds.
> C: It is then stationary for another 50 seconds.
> D: Then it decelerates.

A: ....

....

Look at the axis labels. What sort of graph is this? What does a horizontal line on a velocity/time graph mean?

B: ....

....

What does an upward slope on a velocity/time graph mean? How long is part B of the journey?

C: ....

....

Read the velocity of the object from the vertical axis.

D: ....

....

State the time taken and say how the velocity changes during this time.

(b) Calculate the distance travelled by the object during part A of the journey. (3 marks)

b Now look at this student response.

i Write ✐ the mistake the student has made when reading from the graph.

....

....

> distance travelled = area under the graph ✔
>
> = 150 s × 15 m/s ✗
>
> = 2250 m ✗

ii Write ✐ the correct distance travelled by the object for part A.

.... s × .... m/s = ... m

Your turn!

It is now time to use what you have learned to answer this question. Remember to read the question thoroughly, looking for clues. Make good use of your knowledge from other areas of physics.

Exam-style question

1 A Segway rider moves forward in a straight line at a constant speed.

(a) Which row of the table shows the correct description of the forces on the Segway?

	vertical direction	horizontal direction
A	balanced forces	balanced forces
B	unbalanced forces	balanced forces
C	balanced forces	unbalanced forces
D	unbalanced forces	unbalanced forces

The speed in the horizontal direction is constant.
Does the Segway move in the vertical direction?

(1 mark)

(b) The rider slows down as she goes uphill. Explain the effect this has on the resultant force on the Segway.

Explain answers need a reason. The speed was constant, but it is now changing as she slows down.

....

....

(2 marks)

(c) Figure 1 shows a distance/time graph of a 5-minute Segway ride.

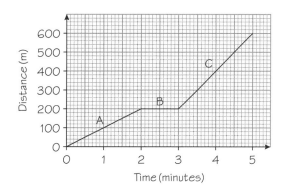

Figure 1

You do not have to calculate the speeds for a **describe** answer. **Compare** means include any similarities and differences in your answer.

(i) Describe and compare the three stages of the journey, A, B and C.

....

....

....

(3 marks)

(ii) Calculate the speed of the Segway in m/s for part A.

Think about the gradient. Look at the units for distance and time. Do any units need converting for the speed to be in m/s?

speed = ... m/s

(4 marks)

Physics

Need more practice?

In the exam, questions about forces and motion could occur as:

- simple standalone questions
- part of a question on forces, work or motion
- part of a question about a practical test.

Have a go at this exam-style question.

Exam-style question

1   A toy car moves 1 m in 3 s at a constant speed. It stops for 2 s, then moves another 1 m in 2 s at a constant speed.

(a) Draw a distance/time graph of this journey on the axes below.

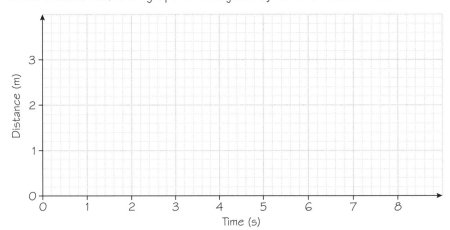

Follow the journey as the time increases. Plot the points and then join them with a ruler.

(3 marks)

(b) Calculate the speed of the toy car, in m/s, for the final 2 s.

speed = ... m/s

(3 marks)

Boost your grade

To improve your grade, practise finding the gradients of distance/time graphs (speed) and velocity/time graphs (acceleration). Also, practise working out the distance travelled by finding the area under velocity/time graphs.

How confident do you feel about each of these **skills?** Colour in the bars.

1 How do I describe the effects of a resultant force?

2 How do I describe distance/time graphs?

3 How do I interpret velocity/time graphs?

③ Electricity

This unit will help you to draw circuits correctly, understand electrical resistance and describe the function of a transformer.

In the exam, you will be asked to tackle questions such as the ones below.

Exam-style questions

1   Draw a circuit diagram to show how the resistance of a lamp could be found in a series circuit.

(3 marks)

2   Which of these is the correct equation for calculating resistance?

⊠   A $R = V \times I$

⊠   B $R = \dfrac{V}{I}$

⊠   C $R = V \times I^2$

⊠   D $R = \dfrac{I}{V}$ (1 mark)

3   Describe the difference between a step-up and a step-down transformer.

....   (2 marks)

You will already have done some work on circuits and resistance. Before starting the **skills boosts**, rate your confidence in each area. Colour in the bars.

1 How do I draw circuits correctly?

2 How do I understand electrical resistance?

3 How do I describe the function of a transformer?

Complete these activities to revise your knowledge of electricity, circuits and resistance.

(1) Match each component to the correct symbol.

One has been done for you on each side.

You need to learn these symbols.

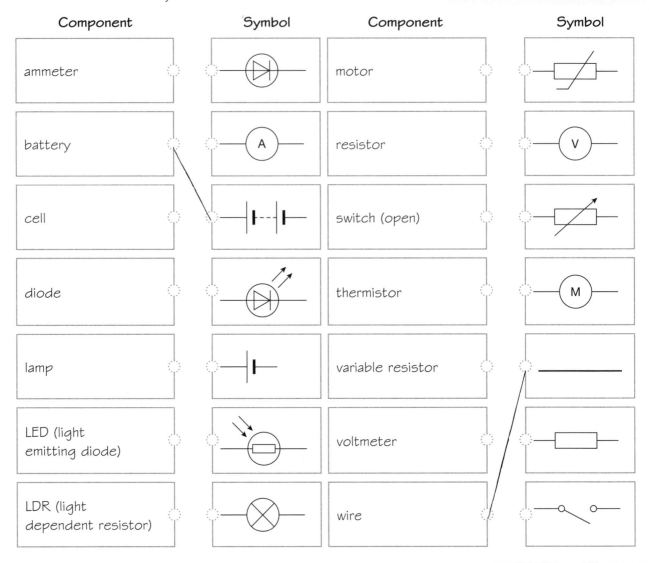

Resistance is related to potential difference and current by this equation:

potential difference (V) = current (A) × resistance (Ω)

$$V = I \times R$$

Learn this! You need to be able to recall, use and rearrange this equation.

(2) Rearrange these word equations, including the units.

(a) current $(A) = $

(b) resistance $(\Omega) = $

(3) What is the function of a transformer?

....

....

1 How do I draw circuits correctly?

Circuit drawings need to show the symbols of the components correctly connected.

(1) Draw ✎ circuit symbols for these components in the spaces below.

A component is a part of an electrical circuit.

a	battery	b	thermistor	c	variable resistor	d	diode	e	resistor

Symbols must be drawn accurately, e.g. (A) not [A] or (a)

(2) Complete ✎ these sentences.

a Current is measured in units called .... (A) using an ammeter. An ammeter is connected in series to measure the current through the circuit.

b Potential difference, or voltage, is measured in units called .... (V) using a voltmeter. A voltmeter is connected in parallel to measure the potential difference across the component.

(3) The first two circuits shown below are correctly connected. The other three circuits are incorrectly connected. Circle (A) the part of each circuit which is incorrectly connected.

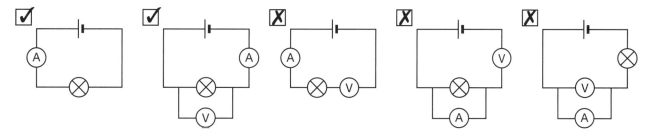

(4) A series circuit contains two cells, one lamp and one motor.

Draw ✎ a circuit diagram that shows how you could measure the potential difference **across**, and the current **through**, the motor.

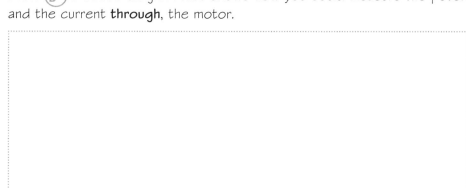

Check you know the correct symbols.

For a current to flow in a circuit there must be **no gaps**.

Which meters do you need? How should they be connected?

Physics

2 How do I understand electrical resistance?

Electrical resistance is a way of saying how difficult it is for electricity to flow through something.

Different components need different potential differences to produce a current through them. The larger the potential difference needed, the larger the **electrical resistance** of the component.

Resistance is measured in units called ohms (Ω).

1 Circle (A) the correct word to complete each sentence.

A higher resistance means a **lower** / **higher** current can flow.

A lower resistance means a **lower** / **higher** current can flow.

For a fixed resistor, the resistance stays the same whatever the potential difference. This graph shows how current changes as potential difference changes for a fixed resistor.

Fixed resistor
The resistance is constant, so the current and voltage are in direct proportion. If two variables are in direct proportion, the graph is a straight line through the origin.

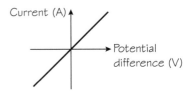

2 For a fixed resistor, if the potential difference doubles, write ✏ what happens to:

a the current ....

b the resistance ....

For a diode and a filament lamp, the resistance changes as the potential difference changes.

These graphs show how current changes as potential difference changes for these components.

Filament lamp
Current and voltage are not in direct proportion as the current causes the filament to heat up. This increases the resistance so the current cannot increase as much when the voltage does.

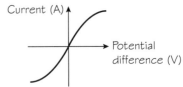

Diode
A diode has a very high resistance in one direction so no current flows that way. Current can only flow in the direction with low resistance.

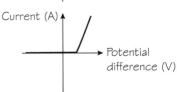

3 Circle (A) the correct words to complete the sentences.

a
Light dependent resistors (LDRs) are used to detect light levels. The resistance decreases as the brightness of the light shining onto the LDR increases. This means **more** / **less** / **the same** current will flow through at a constant voltage in brighter light.

b
Thermistors are used as temperature sensors. The resistance decreases as the temperature increases. This means **more** / **less** / **the same** current will flow through at a constant voltage when it's colder.

3 How do I describe the function of a transformer?

A transformer is a device that can change the voltage (potential difference) of an electricity supply.

Electricity comes from power stations to our homes and other buildings through a network of cables and wires called the **national grid**.

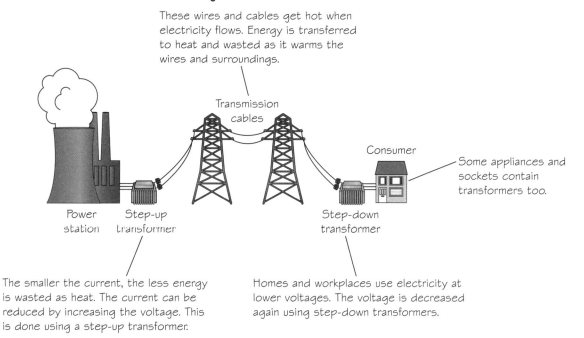

These wires and cables get hot when electricity flows. Energy is transferred to heat and wasted as it warms the wires and surroundings.

Transmission cables

Consumer

Some appliances and sockets contain transformers too.

Power station

Step-up transformer

Step-down transformer

The smaller the current, the less energy is wasted as heat. The current can be reduced by increasing the voltage. This is done using a step-up transformer.

Homes and workplaces use electricity at lower voltages. The voltage is decreased again using step-down transformers.

(1) a What does a step-up transformer do to voltage? ....

b Explain why this is done. ....

....

(2) a What does a step-down transformer do to voltage? ....

b Explain why this is done. ....

....

The diagrams below show the structure of a step-up and step-down transformer. The voltage in the primary coil induces a voltage in the secondary coil by **electromagnetic induction**.

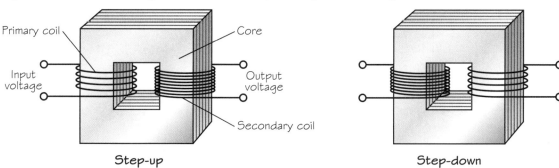

Primary coil

Core

Input voltage

Output voltage

Secondary coil

Step-up

Step-down

(3) Describe how these two transformers are different.

Look carefully at the number of turns in the coils of wire.

....

....

Physics

Sample response

Use these example student responses to improve your understanding. Consider if circuits and symbols are correctly drawn and remind yourself how to calculate resistance.

Exam-style question

1 Calculate the resistance of a lamp in a series circuit with a potential difference of 6 V and a current of 0.6 A.

(3 marks)

1 **a** Annotate ✏ these responses to the question above. What have they got right? What have they got wrong?

To gain the three marks you will need to:
write out the correct equation [1];
put the correct values into the equation [1];
correctly calculate the answer including the unit [1].

A
resistance = voltage × current
= 6V × 0.6A
= 3.6 Ω

B
resistance = voltage/current
= 0.6A/6V
= 0.1

b Now write ✏ your own response. Try to get full marks.

....

....

....

....

....

Exam-style question

2 Draw the circuit you would use to investigate the resistance of a variable resistor.   (3 marks)

2 Circle Ⓐ the errors on this answer and draw ✏ a correct circuit diagram.

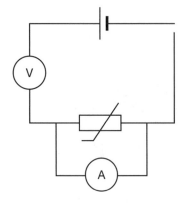

Your turn!

It is now time to use what you have learned to answer the question below. Remember to read the question thoroughly, looking for clues. Make good use of your knowledge from other areas of physics.

1   Draw a circuit diagram to show how the resistance of a lamp could be found in a series circuit.

(3 marks)

Remember Use the correct symbols and leave no gaps in the circuit.

1 **a** What two quantities do you need to know to calculate the resistance? What meters do you use to measure these quantities? How are the meters connected in the circuit?

Quantity	Measured using	Connected in

b Now answer the question.

2   Which of these is the correct equation for calculating resistance?

A $R = V \times I$

B $R = \dfrac{V}{I}$

C $R = V \times I^2$

D $R = \dfrac{I}{V}$

Write out the word equation and rearrange it if you need to.

(1 mark)

3   Describe the difference between the function of a step-up and a step-down transformer.

Function means what it does.

Think about what step-up and step-down mean.

(2 marks)

Physics

Need more practice?

In the exam, questions about electricity could occur as:
- simple standalone questions
- part of a question on electricity, circuits or electromagnetism
- part of a question about a practical test.

Have a go at these exam-style questions.

Exam-style questions

1   Draw a parallel circuit with two cells, one lamp and one motor.

(4 marks)

2   A variable resistor is connected to a 12 V power supply.

   (a) Calculate the current that will flow when the resistance is 3 Ω.

(3 marks)

   (b) Describe what happens to the current when the resistance is increased.

   ....

   ....

(1 mark)

Boost your grade

Make sure you learn the circuit symbols, definitions of key words and the equations you need to calculate resistance. To improve your grade, you could practise calculations using the equation:

$$P = V_p \times I_p = V_s \times I_s$$

This equation involves the power supplied to the primary coil and transferred away from the secondary coil of a transformer.

How confident do you feel about each of these **skills**? Colour in the bars.

1 How do I draw circuits correctly?

2 How do I understand electrical resistance?

3 How do I describe the function of a transformer?

④ Using SI units

This unit will help you to use the correct SI units, to convert between units and to record measurements correctly.

In the exam, you will be asked to tackle questions such as the ones below.

Exam-style questions

1   Calculate the kinetic energy of a ball with a mass of 50 g travelling at a velocity of 5 m/s. Include the unit.

Use the equation $KE = \frac{1}{2}mv^2$

KE = ...

(4 marks)

2   There is a current of 0.8 A in a circuit.

Calculate how much charge flows through the circuit in 5 minutes.

charge = ...C

(4 marks)

You will already have done some work on SI units. Before starting the **skills boosts**, rate your confidence in each area. Colour in 🖉 the bars.

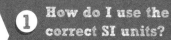

① How do I use the correct SI units?

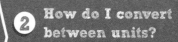

② How do I convert between units?

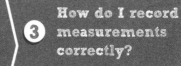

③ How do I record measurements correctly?

SI units are an agreed international system of units, which make sharing scientific information easier.

The table below shows the quantities that have SI units, along with the name and symbol of each unit. Learn this information!

Quantity	Unit	Unit symbol
distance	metre	m
mass	kilogram	kg
time	second	s
current	ampere (amp)	A
temperature	kelvin	K
frequency	hertz	Hz
force	newton	N
energy	joule	J
power	watt	W
pressure	pascal	Pa
electric charge	coulomb	C
electric potential difference	volt	V
electric resistance	ohm	Ω

It is important to write unit symbols with the correct capital or lowercase letters.

① Complete ✐ these sentences using the table. One has been done for you.

    a   Pressure is measured in ....*pascals*........................ (....*Pa*........)

                                                The symbol is put in brackets when there is no number or quantity.

    b   Mass is measured in .... (....................).

    c   .... is measured in .... (N).

    d   .... is measured in hertz (....................).

    e   Electric charge is measured in .... (....................).

② Now complete ✐ the sentences below, using the remaining quantities in the table.

    a   .... is measured in .... (....................).

    b   .... is measured in .... (....................).

    c   .... is measured in .... (....................).

    d   .... is measured in .... (....................).

    e   .... is measured in .... (....................).

    f   .... is measured in .... (....................).

    g   .... is measured in .... (....................).

    h   .... is measured in .... (....................).

1 How do I use the correct SI units?

You need to learn and use the SI units. Always use them unless you are told to use, measure or calculate in other units.

1 Circle Ⓐ the SI units in the box below.

> centimetres   grams   hours   kilograms   kilometres
>
> metres   millimetres   minutes   seconds

2 Circle Ⓐ the SI unit symbols in the box below.

> kg   km   cm   m   s   km/h   pA   hZ   Hz
>
> PA   Pa   HZ   n   N   KG   M   c   C

Whenever you learn an equation, you must learn the correct units and symbols for each quantity in the equation. For example:

$$\text{power (watt, W)} = \frac{\text{work done (joule, J)}}{\text{time taken (second, s)}}$$

3 Write 🖉 the following equations using SI units and symbols.

a $\text{speed} = \dfrac{\text{distance}}{\text{time}}$

b wave speed = frequency × wavelength

c electrical power = current × potential difference

Make sure you can do this for all the equations you need to learn for your course.

Physics

② How do I convert between units?

Units are found wherever there is data, such as in graphs, results tables and calculations.

Unless a question tells you to do something different, calculations should be done using SI units. Sometimes, you will need to convert the units you are given in a question.

① The SI unit for time is seconds (s). Values for time are sometimes given in hours or minutes.

Remember
60 seconds = 1 minute;
60 minutes = 1 hour

a **i** Convert 1.5 hours to minutes.

....

ii Convert 45 minutes to hours.
Give your answer as a decimal.

$\text{hours} \times 60 = \text{minutes}; \dfrac{\text{minutes}}{60} = \text{hours}$

....

b **i** Convert 3 hours to seconds.

$\text{hours} \times 60 \times 60 = \text{seconds};$
$\text{minutes} \times 60 = \text{seconds}$

....

ii Convert 30 minutes to seconds.

....

② Common prefixes in front of units are shown in the table below.

Prefix	Symbol	Value
milli	m (e.g. mm)	1 thousandth $\left(\frac{1}{1000}\right)$ 10^{-3}
centi	c (e.g. cm)	1 hundredth $\left(\frac{1}{100}\right)$ 10^{-2}
kilo	k (e.g. km)	1 thousand (1000) 10^{3}

To convert bigger units to smaller units. multiply

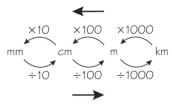

To convert smaller units to bigger units, divide

a Convert 2.6 kW to watts. ....

1 kilowatt (kW) = 1000 watts (W)
kW × 1000 = W

b **i** Convert 86 mm to metres.

1 metre = 1000 millimetres (mm)
 or 100 centimetres (cm)
$\dfrac{mm}{1000} = m, \dfrac{cm}{100} = m$

....

ii Convert 86 cm to metres.

....

3 How do I record measurements correctly?

We use meters and measuring instruments to measure quantities and record values with the correct units. For example, a forcemeter measures force in newtons (N).

1 Look at these two ammeters. Circle Ⓐ the main difference between them.

2 Rulers usually have two scales on them.

a Tick ✓ the scale we normally use for measuring length.

☐ 0 to 30 cm

☐ 0 to 12 inches

Think about the SI unit for length.

b Explain your choice. 🖉

....

....

3 Look at the reading on this stopwatch.

seconds 1/10th seconds

minutes

1/100th seconds

There is more than one unit of time here. Convert the reading to seconds.

reading = ... s

The answer will have 2 decimal places.

Remember 1 minute = 60 seconds

Physics

Sample response

Use these example student responses to improve your understanding. Check that the correct SI units are used and any conversions have been done if needed.

Exam-style question

1 What is the reading on the voltmeter?

[X] A   12.0 V

[X] B   10.2 mV

[X] C   12.0 mV

[X] D   20 V

(1 mark)

---

(1) What mistake has this student made?

....

Exam-style question

2 A car travels at 50 km per hour for 15 minutes. Calculate how far it travels.

Use the equation, speed = $\dfrac{\text{distance}}{\text{time}}$

distance = ... km   **(4 marks)**

---

(2) Look at the student response below. This answer would only gain 1 mark.

distance = speed × time
= 50 × 15
= <u>750 km</u>

Is 750 km a realistic distance for a car to travel in 15 minutes?

Remember The SI unit for distance is metres and the SI unit for time is seconds.

a **i** What unit has the student used for time? ....

ii What has the student done wrong?

....

b The speed is given in kilometres per hour. The question asks for the answer in kilometres. As long as the same units for time are used throughout, the calculation can be done correctly.

Convert the time in minutes to hours so that all the times are in the same unit.

....

c Now complete the calculation.

Your turn!

It is now time to use what you have learned to answer the questions below. Remember to read the questions thoroughly, looking for clues. Make good use of your knowledge from other areas of physics.

Exam-style questions

1   Calculate the kinetic energy of a ball with a mass of 50 g travelling at a velocity of 5 m/s. Include the unit.

Use the equation $KE = \frac{1}{2}mv^2$

$KE =$ ....

(4 marks)

Highlight the values and units given in the question.
Do any units need converting?

2   There is a current of 0.8 A in a circuit.

Calculate how much charge flows through the circuit in 5 minutes.

charge = ... C

(4 marks)

Again, highlight the values and units given in the question.
Check whether any units need converting.
Then start by writing the equation to calculate charge.

The unit for charge is given in the answer space.

Need more practice?

In the exam, questions about SI units could occur as:

- simple standalone questions
- part of a question on any physics topic, especially calculations
- part of a question about a practical test.

Have a go at these exam-style questions.

Exam-style questions

1   Which row of the table is correct?

	measuring instrument	SI unit
A	ruler	length
B	ammeter	amps
C	ruler	cm
D	voltmeter	current

(1 mark)

2   Calculate the current in a washing machine with a power rating of 2 kW. The supply voltage is 230 V.

Use the equation: electrical power = current × potential difference.

Current = ... A

(4 marks)

Boost your grade

To improve your grade, make sure you know all the SI units and how to convert them. Always include units when you record measurements and draw tables and graphs. Practise and learn these skills as units are used a lot in physics.

How confident do you feel about each of these **skills?** Colour in the bars.

1 How do I use the correct SI units?

2 How do I convert between units?

3 How do I record measurements correctly?

⑤ Calculations

This unit will help you learn how to choose the correct equation to do a calculation. You will also learn how to rearrange equations if you need to, and how to set out a calculation to gain maximum marks.

In the exam, you will be asked to tackle questions such as the ones below.

Exam-style questions

1   A car is travelling with a velocity of 18 m/s. It takes 3 seconds to stop.

Calculate the acceleration of the car as it comes to a stop.

Include the unit.

acceleration = ...   (4 marks)

2   A spring with a spring constant of 50 N/m is stretched by 10 cm.

Calculate the energy transferred.

Use one of the equations you have learned.

energy transferred = ...J   (4 marks)

You will already have done some work on calculations. Before starting the **skills boosts**, rate your confidence in each area. Colour in 🖉 the bars.

① **How do I choose and use the correct equation?**

② **How do I rearrange equations?**

③ **How do I set out calculations correctly for physics?**

When you are asked to **calculate** in physics, you need to work out a numerical answer and show the relevant working. This can include using an equation. If the answer has a unit, you need to include this.

1 You should have learned several different equations. Answer the questions below by choosing an equation that contains all of the quantities from the question.

These first two equations come from the list of equations that you need to learn.

a Write ✎ the equation that relates wave speed, frequency and wavelength.
Give your answer in:

   i words: ....

   ii symbols: ....

b Write ✎ the equation that relates density, mass and volume.
Give your answer in:

   i words: ....

   ii symbols: ....

This equation comes from the list of equations that you will be given in the exam.

c Write ✎ the equation that relates energy transferred, current, potential difference and time.
Give your answer in:

   i words: ....

   ii symbols: ....

2 Write ✎ the correct symbol for each of these quantities.

It is important to use lowercase and capital letters correctly.
Some of the equations on the formula sheet include the symbol Δ (the Greek letter delta). This means change, e.g. Δh means change in height.

a acceleration   ....

b current   ....

c density   ....

d frequency   ....

e force   ....

f kinetic energy   ....

g potential difference   ....

h speed (or velocity)   ....

i volume   ....

Some quantities have the same symbol.

j weight   ....

3 Draw ✎ lines to match each quantity with the unit it is measured in.

acceleration	m/s
density	N/m
spring constant	kg/m³
wave speed	m/s²

1 How do I choose and use the correct equation?

In the exam, you will be expected to use many different equations. The equation you need will sometimes be given in the question but there are a lot of equations you will need to learn. The best way to learn the equations is to practise using them as much as you can.

There are four equations involving power:

- power = (current)^2 × resistance
- power = $\dfrac{\text{energy transferred}}{\text{time taken}}$

- power = current × potential difference
- power = $\dfrac{\text{work done}}{\text{time taken}}$

If you are asked to calculate power, how do you decide which equation to use?

Look at the questions below. Choose the correct power equation to use by looking at the quantities in each question and matching them to one of the equations above.

1 **a** Calculate the power of a torch that has a current of 10 A and a potential difference of 3 V.

    i Circle Ⓐ the three quantities in the question.

    ii Which equation contains these three quantities? 🖉

....

   b Calculate the power of a cyclist who transfers 9 kJ of energy in 120 seconds.

    i Circle Ⓐ the three quantities in the question.

    ii Which equation contains these three quantities? 🖉

> Which quantity is measured in seconds?

....

2 **a** Complete the sentence to include the missing quantities.

> Calculate the power of a device that has a .... of 30 Ω and a
>
> .... of 5 A through it.

   b Which equation would you use to calculate the power of the device? 🖉

....

3 **a** Write 🖉 the two equations that involve charge (Q).

> Check your equations sheet.
> Take care: thermal energy is also Q.

....

....

   b Write 🖉 the equation you would use to answer the following question:

Calculate how much charge is moved when a current of 15 A flows for 500 seconds.

....

   c Why did you choose this equation?

....

② How do I rearrange equations?

You may be asked to calculate a quantity that is not the subject of the equation. In this case, you will need to rearrange the equation. In science, we often use the triangle method to rearrange equations.

This table shows how to use the triangle method.

Type of equation	$A = B \times C$	$A = \dfrac{B}{C}$
Type of triangle to use	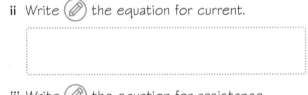 triangle with A over $B \times C$	triangle with B over $A \times C$
Example	wave speed, v = frequency, f × wavlength, λ triangle with v over $f \times \lambda$	power, $P = \dfrac{\text{work done, } E}{\text{time taken, } t}$ triangle with E over $P \times t$

Once you have drawn your triangle, you can use it to rearrange the formula. Simply cover the quantity you want to find, and the triangle will show you whether to multiply or divide the other quantities.

Example	• $v = f \times \lambda$ • $f = \dfrac{v}{\lambda}$ • $\lambda = \dfrac{v}{f}$	• $P = \dfrac{E}{t}$ • $E = P \times t$ • $t = \dfrac{E}{P}$

Use the triangle method to answer the questions below.

① **a** The equation for potential difference is: potential difference, V = current, I × resistance, R

    i Draw 🖉 a triangle for this equation.

    ii Write 🖉 the equation for current.

    iii Write 🖉 the equation for resistance.

b The equation for density is: density, $\rho = \dfrac{\text{mass, } m}{\text{volume, } V}$

    i Draw 🖉 a triangle for this equation.

    ii Write 🖉 the equation for mass.

    iii Write 🖉 the equation for volume.

You must write out the equation for the quantity you want to calculate, not just the triangle. It can be in words or symbols.

3 How do I set out calculations correctly for physics?

Calculation questions in physics are usually worth 3 or 4 marks. You can get marks for using the correct method, even if your final answer is wrong.

Look at the exam-style question and sample student answer below.

Exam-style question

1   Calculate the kinetic energy of a bird with a mass of 35 g flying at 5 m/s.

   Use the equation: kinetic energy $= \frac{1}{2} \times m \times v^2$ **(4 marks)**

Marks for this question would be awarded as follows:

$\frac{35\,g}{1000} = 0.035\,kg$ ⟵ ———————— correct conversion   **(1 mark)**

Note that the mass is given in g. You need to convert the mass to kg before working out your answer.

kinetic energy $= \frac{1}{2} \times 0.035\,kg \times (5\,m/s)^2$ ⟵ correct substitution **(1 mark)**

$\qquad\qquad = \frac{1}{2} \times 0.035 \times 5^2$

$\qquad\qquad = 0.4375\,J$ ⟵ ———————— correct calculation   **(1 mark)**
                                    and unit   **(1 mark)**

Remember You need to square the velocity ($v^2 = v \times v$) and multiply by $\frac{1}{2}$.

Now try this question.

1   Calculate the distance travelled in m by a car moving at a constant speed of 20 m/s for 3 minutes.

   a   Highlight 🖉 the quantities and units in the question.

   b   Do you need to convert any of the units to SI units? If so, which one(s)? 🖉

   ....

   c   Write 🖉 the equation you would use to calculate the distance travelled.

   distance travelled = ...

   d   Substitute 🖉 the correct values into the equation and calculate the answer. Remember to convert to SI units if you need to.

distance = ... m

Sample response

Use these example student responses to improve the way you answer this type of question. Remember to check the quantities to choose the correct equation, consider if it needs rearranging and write out calculations in full.

Exam-style question

1 Calculate the force needed to give an object with a mass of 500 g an acceleration of 10 m/s².

.... **(4 marks)**

m/s² is the unit. This does not mean you need to square the value.

(1) Look at the marked sample answers below and identify where they went wrong. 🖉

Think about the following questions:

- Highlight the quantities in the question. Which equation links these quantities?
- What are the values for mass and acceleration? Is mass given in kg and acceleration in m/s²? If not, what do you need to do?
- Has the unit for force been given or does it need to be included?

a Sample answer A:
$$force = mass \times acceleration = 500 \times 10 = 5000$$
(1 mark)

b Sample answer B:
$$0.5 \times 10 \times 10 = 50\,N$$
(2 marks)

c Sample answer C:
$$force = mass \times acceleration = 0.5 \times 10 = 50\,N$$
(3 marks)

Sample answer C is wrong, but the student would still gain 3 marks because the working is correct.

(2) Now complete 🖉 the calculation yourself so you get 4 marks.

Your turn!

It is now time to use what you have learned to answer this question. Remember to read the question thoroughly, looking for clues. Make good use of your knowledge from other areas of physics.

Exam-style question

1   A car is travelling with a velocity of 18 m/s.
    It takes 3 seconds to stop.

    Calculate the acceleration of the car as it comes to a stop.
    Include the unit.   **(4 marks)**

1 **a** Highlight ✐ the quantities you are given in the question.

   b Do you need to convert any of the quantities into other units? ✐ ....

   c What are you asked to calculate? ✐ ....

   d Do you need to include the units with the answer or are they given? ✐

   ....

2 **a** Write ✐ the equation you need to use to answer this question.

   b Substitute in the values from the question. Remember to make sure you are using the correct units. ✐

   c Complete the calculation and write your answer. ✐

3 Now try this one, using the hints from above. ✐

Exam-style question

2   A spring with a spring constant of 50 N/m is stretched by 10 cm.

    Calculate the energy transferred. Use one of the equations you have learned.

    energy transferred = ... J

                                                                                          (4 marks)

Need more practice?

In the exam, questions about calculations could occur as:

- simple standalone questions
- part of a question on any topic
- part of a question about a practical test.

Have a go at these exam-style questions.

Exam-style questions

1 Which two variables do you need to measure to calculate density?

☐ A mass and potential difference

☐ B weight and volume

☐ C mass and volume

☐ D weight and velocity   (1 mark)

2 A ball with a mass of 0.5 kg is kicked with a force of 12 N.

(a) State the equation that relates force, mass and acceleration.

.... (1 mark)

(b) Calculate the acceleration of the ball in m/s².

acceleration = ... m/s²   (3 marks)

Boost your grade

Using a formula like $KE = \frac{1}{2}mv^2$ can be more challenging than using one like $V = IR$. Learn and practise rearranging all the equations you need to be able to use. Write all calculations out as shown until it becomes automatic.

How confident do you feel about each of these **skills?** Colour in 🖉 the bars.

1 How do I choose and use the correct equation?

2 How do I rearrange equations?

3 How do I set out calculations correctly for physics?

⑥ Graphs

This unit will help you to plot graphs and use them to describe relationships between different variables.

In the exam, you will be asked to tackle questions such as the one below.

Exam-style question

1   A student investigates how the current through a resistor changes as the potential difference across it is changed. The results are shown in the table below.

potential difference (V)	current (A)
0	0
1	0.01
2	0.02
3	0.03
4	0.04
5	0.05

Draw a graph of these results on the grid.

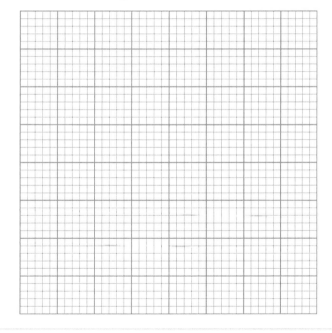

(3 marks)

You will already have done some work on graphs. Before starting the **skills boosts**, rate your confidence in each area. Colour in 🖉 the bars.

1 **How do I plot a graph?**

2 **How do I draw lines of best fit?**

3 **How do I describe the relationship shown by a graph?**

Physics

Graphs are used to represent data and show relationships between variables. You are expected to be able to draw graphs accurately and to make conclusions from them.

This table shows the graph types used in physics.

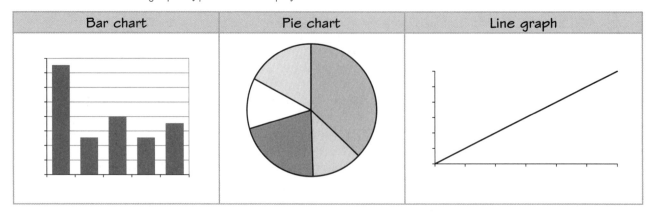

Bar chart	Pie chart	Line graph

The most commonly used graph in physics is the line graph. It shows the relationship between two continuous variables. A continuous variable is one that can have any value and can be measured, e.g. time.

1 List ✎ six other continuous variables used in physics.

....

....

The independent variable (the variable that has been controlled and changed in the experiment) goes on the horizontal axis (↔). The dependent variable (the variable that is then measured) goes on the vertical axis (↕).

2 Label ✎ the axes for the graphs below. The first one has been done for you.

a A graph showing how the speed (m/s) of a vehicle changes over time (s).

b A graph showing how the pressure (Pa) of a gas changes with temperature (K).

c A graph showing how the angle of refraction (°) changes as the angle of incidence(°) is increased.

Remember to add the units.

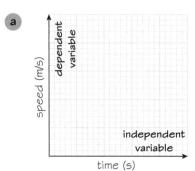

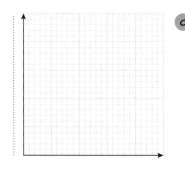

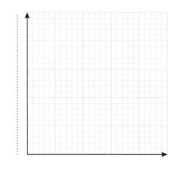

For questions where you are asked to draw a graph, you will usually get:
- 1 mark for plotting the points correctly
- 1 mark for labelling and using an accurate scale
- 1 mark for a straight or curved line of best fit.

If you are given a graph to interpret, you could get marks for:
- describing the relationship between the variables
- reading values from the graph
- identifying anomalous points that don't fit the pattern.

1 How do I plot a graph?

To 'plot' a graph means to produce a graph by marking points accurately on a grid and then drawing a line of best fit through these points. You must include a suitable scale and appropriately labelled axes if these are not provided in the question.

Step 1: Choose a scale:

- Look at the range of values you need to plot, i.e. the lowest and highest values.
- Make sure your graph fills at least half the height and width of the grid given.
- It is easiest to go up in intervals of 1, 2, 5 or 10.

The diagram below shows the best way to fit a range up to 80 s on the grid. It is usual to make your scale slightly longer than needed so this scale goes up to 100 s.

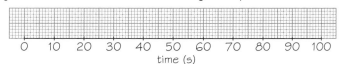

Remember to use an accurate scale and label it correctly.

① **a** You have a set of values from 0 s to 20 s. Add a suitable scale to the axis below.

b You have a set of values from 0 s to 5 s. Add a suitable scale to the axis below. ✎

Step 2: Plot the data points:

- Plot each point as a small neat cross, using a sharp pencil.
- Your points should be accurate to +/− half a small square.
- Find the value on the x-axis (the horizontal axis) first, and then go up to the value on the y-axis.

② Look at the diagram on the right. This shows how to plot the point (2, 27).

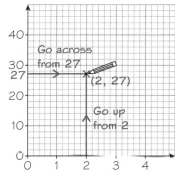

③ **a** What value does each small square have on the horizontal scale? ✎ ....

b What value does each small square have on the vertical scale? ✎ ....

④ Now plot these points on the grid.

(1, 22)

(2.8, 6)

(3.5, 33)

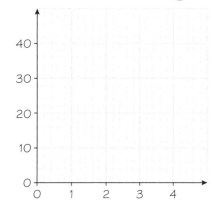

Physics

2 How do I draw lines of best fit?

Lines of best fit can be straight or curved. Some will pass through all of the points, while others will have an even spread of points on either side. There is usually no right or wrong line, but the guidelines below will help you to draw the best one you can.

To draw a line of best fit:

- Draw a single line in pencil.
- For straight lines, use a transparent ruler so you can see all the points.
- Avoid 'tram lines' or double lines.
- Only use dot-to-dot lines for distance/time and velocity/time graphs.

(1) Look at the examples below and draw ✐ a line or curve of best fit on each graph.

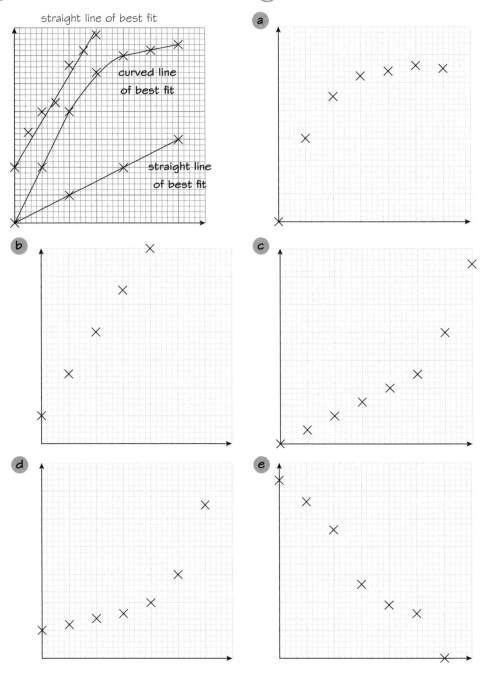

Can you draw a straight line that passes through all the points? If not, can you draw a curve that passes through all the points? Can you draw a line or curve that passes through most of the points?

If your line of best fit has a straight section and a curved section, use a ruler to draw the straight section.

③ How do I describe the relationship shown by a graph?

To describe the relationship shown by a graph, state how the dependent variable (vertical scale) changes as the independent variable (horizontal scale) changes. This could include stating how the steepness of the line or curve changes and what this means.

This table shows the different types of graph.

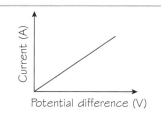	• **Straight line** graphs show a **linear** relationship. • If a graph has a **straight line through the origin**, this shows that the two quantities plotted are **directly proportional**. • In this graph, current **increases** as potential difference **increases**. The graph has a **positive** gradient. • The gradient is constant (a straight line). This shows that the current increases at a constant rate.
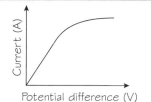	• Some graph lines are **curved**. • In this graph, potential difference **increases** as current **increases** (as before). However, the gradient is not constant: the line gradually becomes less steep and starts to level off. This shows that the current is increasing at a slower rate.
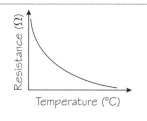	• This graph shows an **inverse** relationship. As the temperature **increases**, the resistance **decreases**. • The line is steeper at lower temperatures. This shows that the resistance decreases quickly at first. • At higher temperatures, the graph line is less steep. This shows that the resistance decreases more slowly as the temperature continues to increase.

Lines of best fit can be used to:

• show anomalies: any points that are a long way from the line may be due to experimental error

• make predictions: you can predict an unmeasured value by reading it off the line.

① Describe 🖉 the relationship shown by each of these graphs.

   a A graph to show how the velocity of a moving object changes with time.

          ....

          ....

          ....

   b A graph to show how current changes as potential difference changes for a diode.

          ....

          ....

          If possible, give values where the graph changes.

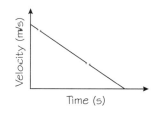

Physics

Sample response

Use these example student responses to improve the way you draw graphs. Look at the variables, scales and units. Check if points are correctly plotted and whether any lines drawn should be straight or curved.

1 Look at each graph and identify the errors the student has made.

Highlight the errors on each graph to help you remember how to draw graphs correctly.

a

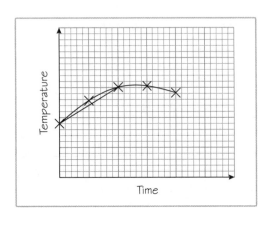

b

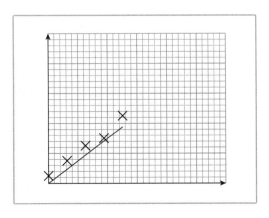

....

....

....

....

....

....

....

....

....

....

....

....

....

....

c This graph is based on the data in the table below.

Identify the errors in the graph.

Angle of incidence (°)	0	10	20	30	40	50
Angle of reflection (°)	0	10	20	30	40	50

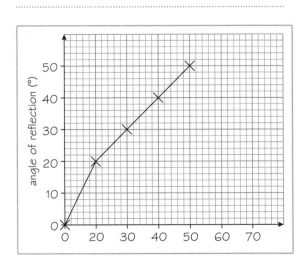

....

....

....

Your turn!

It is now time to use what you have learned to answer the question below. Remember to read the question thoroughly, looking for clues. Make good use of your knowledge from other areas of physics.

Exam-style question

1   A student investigates how the current through a resistor changes as the potential difference across it is changed. The results are shown in the table below.

potential difference (V)	current (A)
0	0
1	0.01
2	0.02
3	0.03
4	0.04
5	0.05

Draw a graph of these results on the grid.   (3 marks)

1   **a**   Which variable goes on the horizontal axis? ✎ ....

    b   Which variable goes on the vertical axis? ✎ ....

    c   Now draw ✎ the graph.

- Look at the maximum and minimum readings for potential difference and current.
- Choose suitable scales for the axes and label the axes, including the units.
- Use a pencil and ruler to draw the axes.
- Plot the points and draw a line of best fit. Do you need a ruler to do this?

In an exam, you will not be asked to describe the relationship shown by a graph you have plotted. However, you will have to do this for practical work.

2   Describe ✎ the relationship shown by the graph you have drawn.

....

....

....

Need more practice?

In the exam, questions about graphs could occur as:

- simple standalone questions
- part of a question on any topic
- part of a question about a practical test.

Have a go at this exam-style question.

1 A student investigates how the extension of a spring changes as the force on it is changed. The results are shown in the table.

force (N)	0	0.4	0.8	1.2	1.6	2.0
extension (cm)	0	2.0	4.0	6.0	8.0	8.5

(a) Draw a graph on the grid to show how the extension changes as the force is increased.

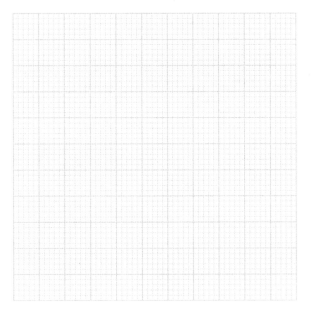

(3 marks)

(b) Describe the relationship shown by the graph.

....

.... (2 marks)

Make sure you plot all graphs accurately to gain maximum marks during investigations and exams. Practise looking at the relationships shown by graphs where the variables are not directly proportional to each other

How confident do you feel about each of these **skills?** Colour in the bars.

1 **How do I plot a graph?**

2 **How do I draw lines of best fit?**

3 **How do I describe the relationship shown by a graph?**

⑦ Answering extended response questions

This unit will help you to answer longer questions by deciding what is being asked and then planning a concise answer with the right amount of detail.

In the exam, you will be asked to tackle questions such as the one below.

Exam-style question

1   Vehicles can be run on fuels such as diesel and bio-fuel.

Assess the suitability of diesel and bio-fuel as fuels to run a vehicle.

....   (6 marks)

You will already have done some work on extended response questions. Before starting the **skills boosts**, rate your confidence in each area. Colour in 🖉 the bars.

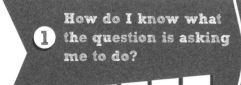

1   How do I know what the question is asking me to do?

2   How do I plan my answer?

3   How do I choose the right detail to answer the question concisely?

Physics

A **command word** is the word at the start of a question that tells you what you are expected to do.

Exam-style question

1 Describe the energy transfers when a ball is thrown up into the air and falls back down.

The table below shows the most commonly used command words for the extended questions.

Command word	Meaning
assess	Give careful consideration to all the factors that apply and choose which are the most important. Come to, and write, a conclusion.
compare	Look for the similarities **or** differences between two (or more) things. You should not need to draw a conclusion. The answer must relate to both (or all) the things mentioned in the question.
compare and contrast	The same as 'compare' but you must include at least one similarity **and** one difference between the things that are being compared.
describe	Give an account of something. Statements need to be developed as they are often linked. You do not need to give reasons.
explain	The answer must have some reasoning and include justifications of the points given.

① Look at the table above.

Write 🖊 the command word that tells you to:

ⓐ include some reasoning ....

ⓑ include both similarities and differences ....

ⓒ write a conclusion ....

ⓓ give an account without any reasons ....

ⓔ give similarities or differences between things ....

How do I know what the question is asking me to do?

The command word is usually at the beginning of the sentence telling you what to do. It is important to know what the command words mean. Use the information given in the question stem to focus on the correct content. You may find it useful to highlight the key words and phrases in the question.

Key words and phrases in the question will tell you the:

- type of answer needed
- content to focus on
- quantities and values needed for equations and calculations.

Look at these extended writing questions and answer the questions that follow.

Exam-style question

1   Compare the properties of alpha, beta and gamma radiation in terms of their:

- range in air
- ability to penetrate through materials
- ability to ionise atoms.   (6 marks)

① Circle Ⓐ the command word. What does this word mean you have to do? 🖉

....

....

② Underline Ⓐ the types of radiation you are asked to compare. How many are there? 🖉

....

③ Highlight 🖉 the properties you are going to write about for each type of radiation.
What are they? 🖉

....

....

....

Exam-style question

1   A girl holds a ball with a mass of 0.2 kg. She throws it upwards at a speed of 4 m/s.
She catches it when it comes back down.

Explain how the energy stored in the ball changes as it is thrown up into the air and
comes back down again.

Include calculations in your answer.

Gravitational field strength, $g = 10$ N/kg   (6 marks)

④ Highlight and label 🖉 the:

   a   command word   b   key phrases

   c   quantities and values needed for the calculations.

2 How do I plan my answer?

Make sure you know what you are being asked to do by using the information given in the question. Then consider what you know about the topic and which parts are relevant to the question. Sometimes the wording of the question can help you to plan your answer.

Consider this question again.

Exam-style question

1   Compare the properties of alpha, beta and gamma radiation in terms of their:

• range in air

• ability to penetrate through materials

• ability to ionise atoms.   (6 marks)

① The boxes below contain information that you may know about the three different types of radiation.

Penetrate means pass through or into. **Ability** means how good it is at doing something.

Use the wording of the exam-style question to identify the parts which are relevant.
Alpha radiation has been done as an example.

Alpha radiation

Alpha particles (α or $^{4}_{2}$He) contain two protons and two neutrons. They are the same as a helium nucleus and have a relative mass of 4. They don't have any electrons in them and have a charge of $+2$. Alpha particles travel at high speeds and are very good at ionising atoms. They can only travel a few cm in air and are stopped by a sheet of paper.

• range in air? .... *alpha particles travel a few cm in air* ....

• ability to penetrate through materials? .... *alpha particles are stopped by a sheet of paper* ....

• ability to ionise atoms? .... *alpha particles are very ionising* ....

Beta radiation

Beta particles (β^- or $^{0}_{-1}$e) are high-speed electrons with high energy. Beta particles are moderately ionising and can penetrate further into materials. They can travel a few metres in air. They have a relative mass of $\frac{1}{1835}$ and a charge of -1. They are stopped by aluminium a few millimetres thick.

• range in air? ....

• ability to penetrate through materials? ....

• ability to ionise atoms? ....

Gamma radiation

Gamma rays (γ) are high frequency electromagnetic waves. They are weakly ionising and can penetrate materials easily. They can travel a few kilometres in air. They need thick lead or several metres of concrete to stop them. They travel at the speed of light.

• range in air? ....

• ability to penetrate through materials? ....

• ability to ionise atoms? ....

3 How do I choose the right detail to answer the question concisely?

The command word will tell you what style of answer you need to write and what should be included. Select the parts of the topic that answer the question and avoid simply writing everything you know.

Exam-style question

1 Compare the properties of alpha, beta and gamma radiation in terms of their:
- range in air
- ability to penetrate through materials
- ability to ionise atoms. (6 marks)

In skills boost 2, you planned your answer by identifying the relevant information. Now you need to put this information together in an organised way that shows your line of reasoning.

You could organise your answer in two ways.

① Focus on one radiation at a time, comparing its properties with the other two.

For example:

> Alpha radiation has the shortest range in air and can only travel a few centimetres. It is stopped by paper so penetrates less than the other radiation types. It is very good at ionising atoms.

The command word 'compare' tells you to include similarities or differences. In this case you need to say how each of the properties is different for the three types of radiation.

Compare the different properties by using comparison words such as more, less, further, shortest, etc.

a Highlight ✐ the words that show a comparison.

The phrase 'very good' is specific to alpha: it does not show how it compares with beta and gamma.

b Now write ✐ a similar paragraph for beta radiation that compares it with alpha and gamma radiation.

....

....

....

② Now focus on one property at a time, using it to compare all three types of radiation. For example:

> Alpha radiation can only travel a few centimetres in air whereas beta radiation can travel a few metres. However, gamma rays can travel a few kilometres in air so go the furthest of them all.

a Highlight ✐ the words that emphasise the comparisons.

b Now write ✐ a similar paragraph about ability to penetrate materials.

....

....

....

Physics

Sample response

Use this sample student response to improve the way you answer this type of question. Use information given in the unit to help you. Consider whether the command word has been properly answered and all the points have been covered in a well organised way.

Exam-style question

1 Compare the properties of alpha, beta and gamma radiation in terms of their:

• range in air

• ability to penetrate through materials

• ability to ionise atoms.

(6 marks)

Student response

Alpha radiation is alpha particles that are helium nuclei which contain two protons and two neutrons and have a relative mass of 4. Alpha particles are very ionising. They cannot penetrate through paper so do not penetrate far. They have a small range in air.

Gamma radiation has the longest range in air and can travel a few kilometres. It can penetrate through most materials and is only stopped by thick lead or several metres of concrete. Gamma rays are the least ionising of the three types of radiation.

Beta radiation has a larger range in air than alpha and can travel a few metres. It is stopped by a few mm of aluminium metal. Beta radiation is high speed electrons with a charge of -1.

(1) Cross out (X) any information that has been written that is not relevant to the question.

(2) Complete (✎) this table to see if all of the points have been covered.
The table has been started for you.

	alpha	beta	gamma
range in air	✓		
penetration			
ionising ability			

(3) Have the three properties been **compared** or **put in order** for all three types of radiation? (A) Yes / No   Look for comparison words.

(4) Has the answer been written in a logical way? (A) Yes / No

(5) Now have a go at answering the question for yourself. If you need more space to write your answer, continue on paper. (✎)

....

....

....

....

....

Your turn!

It is now time to use what you have learned to answer the question below. Remember to read the question thoroughly, looking for clues. Make good use of your knowledge from other areas of physics.

Exam-style question

1   Vehicles can be run on fuels such as diesel and bio-fuel.

   Assess the suitability of diesel and bio-fuel as fuels to run a vehicle.   **(6 marks)**

The following information may help you to plan your answer:

> Diesel is a fossil fuel made from oil. It is a non-renewable energy resource which will run out one day. Burning fossil fuels releases carbon dioxide and other gases into the atmosphere. Carbon dioxide contributes to climate change on Earth. Diesel is good to use in vehicles because it stores a lot of energy and is easy to store and transport. Diesel releases particulates that cause air pollution and has also been associated with respiratory problems in people.
>
> Bio-fuels come from plants or animal waste. They can be made from wood or from the parts of plants that are not eaten. Some crops are grown specifically to be made into bio-fuels. This can cause problems because of a lack of bio-diversity. Also, it removes land space used to grow food crops, and can have an effect on food prices. Bio-fuels can be used in the same ways as fossil fuels. They also release carbon dioxide when they burn, but are considered more carbon neutral as plants remove carbon dioxide from the atmosphere when they grow. However, energy is also needed to grow, transport, and turn them into fuel.

(1) Start by planning your answer.

   a   Highlight ✐ the command word. What does this mean you need to do?

   ....

   ....

   b   Read the passage above and highlight ✐ the key information that will help you to answer the question.

   c   Think about how to organise your ideas. Will you write about diesel first then bio-fuel, as in the question? Or will you consider one factor for both fuels at the same time?

   ....

   ....

(2) Now write ✐ your answer on a separate sheet of paper. Make sure you compare the two fuels rather than simply writing down all the information you highlighted in b .

(3) Check your answer and circle Ⓐ the correct answer to each of the following questions.

   a   Have you used comparison words? **Yes** / **No**

   b   Have you organised your ideas logically? **Yes** / **No**

   c   Have you used scientific ideas and scientific language correctly? **Yes** / **No**

   d   Have you included a conclusion which says which fuel is the most suitable and why? **Yes** / **No**

Need more practice?

In the exam, extended response questions could be asked about any physics topic from the specification or about an experimental procedure.

Have a go at this exam-style question.

Exam-style question

1   A girl holds a ball with a mass of 0.2 kg. She throws it upwards at a speed of 4 m/s. She catches it when it comes back down.

Explain how the energy stored in the ball changes as it is thrown up into the air and comes back down again.

Include calculations in your answer.

Gravitational field strength, $g = 10$ N/kg

....

....

....

....

....

....

....

....

....

....

....

....

(6 marks)

Boost your grade

Practise answering extended response questions using different command words. You could also try writing your own questions to help you test your knowledge of a topic.

How confident do you feel about each of these **skills?** Colour in the bars.

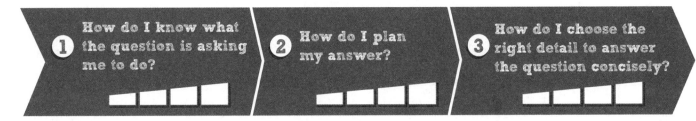

1 How do I know what the question is asking me to do?

2 How do I plan my answer?

3 How do I choose the right detail to answer the question concisely?

Answers

Biology

Unit 1

Page 2
1. Arrow from right to left
2. Water (small blue molecules)
3. Concentration falls
4. A

Page 3
1. B

Exam-style question

1. (a) Left-hand side
   (b) Right-hand side
   (c) Carbon dioxide to the left and oxygen to the right
   (d) There is a higher concentration of oxygen on the left. Oxygen molecules will move (diffuse) towards the area with a lower concentration, down the concentration gradient.

Page 4

1. a

	Distilled	10% sucrose	20% sucrose
Change in mass (g)	$11 - 10 = 1\,g$	$10 - 10 = 0\,g$	$9 - 10 = -1\,g$
% change in mass	$\frac{1}{10} \times 100 = +10\%$	$\frac{0}{10} \times 100 = 0\%$	$\frac{-1}{10} \times 100 = -10\%$

   b. The piece placed in distilled water
   c. This is the same concentration as the inside of the potato cells. There will be no net movement of water molecules in either direction so there is no change in mass.
   d. An actual change in mass of 1 g would be a huge change if the initial mass was 2 g, but a very small change if the initial mass was 100 g. The percentage change gives an idea of the size of the change even if you do not know the initial mass. It also allows you to compare the changes in substances with different initial masses.

Page 5
1. transporter protein; energy; against/up

2.

Transport process	Molecules move down the concentration gradient?	Uses energy from respiration?	Molecules move against the concentration gradient?
Diffusion	✓	✗	✗
Osmosis	✓	✗	✗
Active transport	✗	✓	✓

Exam-style question

1. (a) The concentration drops to 0.
   (b) Molecules are moved from low concentration to higher concentration, against the concentration gradient. Energy from respiration is used.

Page 6
1. a. The response is a description, not an explanation.
   b. Osmosis

c. There is a higher salt concentration in the sea water so water moves out of the plant roots by osmosis.

2. There is a plant absorbs mineral ions by active transport.
   They are used to build proteins / cell membranes / for photosynthesis / for respiration.

Page 7
Exam-style question

Substance entering or leaving cell	How the substance crosses the cell membrane
Minerals entering a plant root from the soil	Enter by active transport: energy from respiration is used to move minerals from a low concentration to a higher concentration in the plant
Oxygen entering a liver cell	Enters by diffusion, from a high concentration to a lower concentration
Water entering a plant root from the soil	Enters by osmosis, from a dilute solution to a more concentrated solution
Glucose taken up from the small intestine	Taken up by active transport, using energy from respiration, so that all the glucose is taken up

(1 mark for each correct row)

Page 8
Exam-style question

1. (a) -10.8 / -7.1 / -5.6 / -2.6 / $+6.3$
   all values correct **(2)**, one or more incorrect **(1)**
   (b) The potato had a higher sugar solution concentration than the surrounding solution **(1)**.
   Water moved from the more dilute solution to the more concentrated solution by osmosis **(1)**, so water moved into into the potato, increasing its mass **(1)**.

Unit 2

Page 10
1. a. C

   b.

2. active site; fit; denatured

Page 11

(1) **a** substrate; product; faster

b 20; 40; 40; 60

(2) **a** a protein

b amino acids

c Proteins are broken down/digested into amino acids by the protein-digesting enzyme (protease).

d Rises steeply at first, then more slowly and then levels off

e As the time increases, the concentration of amino acids rises quickly at first to approximately 22.5 mg/dm³ at 10 minutes. Then, for the next 10 minutes, the reaction slows down and the concentration increases more slowly, up to 28.0 mg/dm³ at 20 minutes. The graph then begins to level off, reaching a concentration of 30.0 mg/dm³ at 30 minutes.

Page 12

(1) **a** At substrate concentration of 2.0 mol/dm³

b When the substrate concentration is zero there are no substrate molecules. Therefore, there will be no collisions and the rate of reaction is zero.

As the substrate concentration increases there are more substrate molecules. Therefore the substrate molecules collide with the enzyme molecules more frequently and the reaction rate is higher.

The highest number of collisions is when the substrate concentration is at 2.0 mol/dm³ so this gives the highest rate of reaction.

(2) **a** C

b A

(3) **a** All the starch has been digested, so there are no collisions.

b The concentration of starch is decreasing, so there are fewer collisions.

Page 13

(1) **a** substrate is hydrogen peroxide; product is oxygen

b very little; very slowly; not very often

c lots of/more; more often

d 40 °C

e It falls to zero

f The enzyme has denatured: this means the active site has changed shape so the substrate will no longer fit into it.

Page 14

(1) There will be more collisions with enzyme molecules so the rate of reaction will be higher.

(2) 50 °C

(3) At low temperatures, the enzyme and substrate molecules do not have much kinetic energy so they do not collide very often. At 50 °C the molecules have more kinetic energy, so they move faster. There are more collisions between enzyme and substrate molecules, so the rate of reaction is faster. At higher temperatures, the enzyme starts to denature. The shape of the active site changes, so the substrate can no longer fit into it. The rate of reaction slows down and eventually stops altogether.

Page 15

Exam-style question

1 **(a)** At pH 2 the rate of digestion is zero **(1)**. As the pH rises, the rate of reaction rises to a maximum of 0.55 s⁻¹ at pH 7 **(1)**. Above pH 7 the rate drops again **(1)**.

(b) pH 7 **(1)**

(c) This is the optimum pH, where the active site fits the substrate **(1)**. At higher and lower pH values, the active site changes shape, so the substrate cannot fit into it **(1)**.

(d) The enzyme was denatured by the low pH **(1)**, so the substrate did not fit the active site **(1)**.

Page 16

Exam-style question

1 **(a)** A catalyst is a substance that speeds up the rate of a reaction without itself being used up **(1)**.

(b)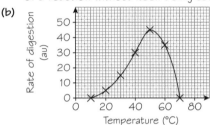

smooth line passing through all points **(1)**

(c) 20–22 **(1)** arbitrary units **(1)**

(d) The enzyme has denatured, so the active site has changed shape **(1)**. The substrate (starch) no longer fits the active site properly **(1)**.

Unit 3

Page 18

(1)

Stage	Correct order
The cell increases in size and increases the number of sub-cellular structures such as ribosomes and mitochondria. DNA replicates to form two copies of each chromosome.	1
The cytoplasm and cell membrane divide to form two identical, daughter cells.	3
A set of chromosomes moves to each end of the cell and the nucleus divides.	2

(2)

(3) **a** The genetic information / DNA / chromosomes is copied / doubled / duplicated.

b The cell membrane and cytoplasm divide to form two new identical daughter cells.

(4)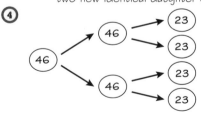

Page 19

(1) **a** A prophase, B metaphase, C anaphase, D telophase

b Cytokinesis

c In B (metaphase) the chromosomes line up across the middle of the cell. In C (anaphase) the chromosome copies are separated and move to opposite ends of the cell.

2 a 360 minutes

b 1 minute

c

	Angle (°)	Time in minutes	Time in hours and minutes
Interphase	320	320 min	5 h 20 min
Mitosis	20	20 min	0 h 20 min
Cytokinesis	20	20 min	0 h 20 min

3 a 20 chromosomes / double / twice as many

b 10 chromosomes (in each daughter cell)

Page 20

1 nucleus 3   gene 1   chromosome 2

2 a mitosis

b It replicates / doubles / is copied / duplicates / is cloned.

c 46

d For growth / repair / replacement of damaged cells

3 Completed diagram should be exactly the same as the original.

Page 21

1 B

2 testes / ovaries

3 BF   Bf   bF   bf

4 halves; non-identical; diploid; haploid; sexual; increases

Page 22

1 There are two ticks in the first row, so the student would not get a mark for this row.

There is no tick in the second row, so the student would not get a mark for that part of the question.

2 Could also add:

Each of the cells is different.

Each cell has half the number of chromosomes of the original cell.

3 Growth requires identical copies of cells to be made. It is mitosis that produces identical cells.

Page 23

Exam-style question

1 (a) (1 mark for each correct row)

Feature	Mitosis or meiosis?
Production of eggs	Meiosis
A lizard growing a new tail	Mitosis
Production of pollen in a flower	Meiosis
Cells replaced on the skin to heal a cut	Mitosis

(b) A man: testes (1)

A woman: ovaries (1)

(c) Mitosis produces identical cells; meiosis produces non-identical cells (1).

Mitosis produces two daughter cells; meiosis produces four gamete cells (1).

Mitosis is for asexual reproduction, growth and repair; meiosis is for sexual reproduction (1).

Mitosis occurs in all body cells except for the testes and ovaries; meiosis occurs only in the testes and ovaries. (1)

(any two points for 2 marks)

Page 24

Exam-style question

1 (a) meiosis (1)

(b) mitosis (1)

(c) zygote / fertilised egg (1)

(d) 4 pg (half) (1)

Unit 4

Page 26

1 a Independent variable: temperature

Dependent variable: height of bubbles

b Experiment is carried out in a water bath at set temperatures

c Same volume of same concentration used in all stages of the experiment; all other volumes the same in all stages

d Always use 2% hydrogen peroxide; keep all volumes the same in all stages

2 Temperature (°C)   Height of bubbles (mm)

Page 27

1 a substrate concentration

b pH

3 a clarity of apple juice

b length of a potato chip

3 a Two from: temperature, pH, concentration of CO_2, type of plant

b Two from: temperature, concentration of all chemicals

4 a speed of air movement

b rate of water loss

c Three from: temperature, size of plant, type of plant, light intensity, availability of water to the plant's roots

Page 28

1 moving the light

2 counting the number of bubbles released per minute

3 a Use a stop watch to time a set amount of time (e.g. 1 minute) and count all the bubbles released in that time.

b Add the same mass of sodium hydrogencarbonate.

4 pondweed; 5 / a few; minute; 3; 4; 20; 30

Page 29

1 Temperature (°C)   Time taken to digest protein (seconds)

2 a light intensity

b Two from: independent variable is in right-hand column; dependent variable is in left-hand column; no units are given

3 a temperature

b rate of water loss

c

Temperature (°C)	Rate of water loss from shoot (g)			
	Trial 1	Trial 2	Trial 3	mean
10				
20				
30				

Page 30

1 They could have stated that it was concentration of food dye.

(**2**) A unit for the spread of dye

(**3**) Two

Page 31

Exam-style question

1 (a) The distance the ruler drops before it is caught **(1)**

(b) Two from: same ruler, same starting point (0 cm mark held between thumb and forefinger), same level of distraction in room around subject, same people being tested *(1 mark for each correct point)*

(c) Different people were tested at different times of day **(1)**; the same person should be tested at different times to see how reaction time is affected by time of day **(1)**.

Page 32

Exam-style question

1 (a) in shade = 2.7 **(1)**; in sun = 5.7 **(1)**

(b) Place the quadrat three times in the sun and three times in the shade **(1)**; state size of quadrat **(1)**; state how position of quadrat was selected (this should be randomly selected) **(1)**.

Unit 5

Page 34

(**1**) (a) How the percentage cover of reeds changes as distance from the pond increases

(b) B

(**2**) (a) 13%

(b) 7 m

(**3**) The percentage cover of reeds is highest close to the pond and decreases as distance from the pond increases. The soil is wetter near the pond. The data show that reed plants prefer wetter conditions.

Page 35

(**1**) (a) 16 cm³/s

(b) 14 cm³/s

(c) 4 mg/dm³

(**2**) (a) values up to 8 mg/dm³

(b) curved, becoming less steep

(c) concentration; increases; 12; straight; constant; curved; 16; 18

Page 36

(**1**) (a) distance of lamp from plant, in cm

(b) rate of photosynthesis, in bubbles per minute

(c) decreases

(d) decreases

(e) curve; falls; 10 cm; less; 35

(f) quickly; 6; slowly; 35

Page 37

(**1**) the effect of changing light intensity on the rate of photosynthesis

(**2**) A

(**3**) The light provides the energy for photosynthesis.

(**4**) photosynthesis; energy; intensity; decreases; decreases; photosynthesis; 35

Page 38

(**1**) the units (%)

(**2**) The chances of dying decrease from 20% to 14%; this is not halving.

(**3**) 2 marks. The student has described the shape of the curve [1 mark], and stated some correct data values

from the graph [1 mark]. However, the student has mistaken coronary heart disease for cancer, and has not correctly explained what the graph shows.

Page 39

Exam-style question

1 (a) For the first 25 hours the graph is a horizontal line, which shows that the bean root is not growing **(1)**. From 25 hours to 100 hours the graph is a curve, rising steeply **(1)**. This shows that the root grows quickly, from 0 mm at 25 hours to 33 mm at 100 hours **(1)**.

(b) 50 mm **(1)**

(c) The seed must absorb water from the surroundings **(1)**, this will activate the enzymes that start to digest its stored food. This allows growth to start **(1)**.

Page 40

Exam-style question

1 (a) As the blood alcohol level increases, the risk of an accident increases. The graph is a curve that rises slowly at first **(1)**. This means that for blood alcohol levels up to about 60 mg per 100 cm³, the risk of an accident increases slowly **(1)**. For blood alcohol levels from about 60 mg per 100 cm³ to 200 mg per 100 cm³, the curve rises more steeply. This means that as the alcohol level rises above 60 mg per 100 cm³ blood, the risk increases more quickly **(1)**.

(b) 4 **(1)**

(c) 120 mg per 100cm³ blood **(1)**

Unit 6

Page 42

(**1**) (a) 30 mm

(b) $\dfrac{30}{6}$

(c) ×5

(**2**) (a) 20 cm³ produced in 5 s

(b) 4 cm³/s in 1 s

(c) 4 cm³/s

(**3**) (a) $\dfrac{4}{15}$

(b) $\dfrac{4}{15}$ = 0.266666

(c) 0.266666 × 100 = 26.6666% = 26.7% (to 1 d.p.)

Page 43

(**1**) (a) length of object = 0.04 mm, length of image = 80 mm

(b) $\dfrac{80}{0.04}$ = 2000

(b) magnification = ×2000

(**2**) (a) actual size = $\dfrac{\text{image size}}{\text{magnification}}$

(b) actual size = $\dfrac{5\ mm}{200}$

(c) actual size = 0.025 mm

Page 44

(**1**) (a) 24 cm³ produced in 3 minutes

(b) divide by 3: 8 cm³ in 1 min

(c) rate of reaction = 8 cm³/minute

(**2**) (a) 8 mm/h

(b) 30 − 24 = 6 mm in 1 hour
rate = 6 mm/h

③ **a** 12 mm growth in 50 hours

b $\dfrac{12\,mm}{50\,hours}$

c rate of growth = 0.24 mm/h

Page 45

① $\dfrac{24}{80} = 0.3 = 30.0\%$

② $\dfrac{29\,435}{45\,692} = 0.6442 = 64.42\% = 64.4\%$ (to 1 d.p.)

③ **a** 385 000 − 345 000 = 40 000

b original value = 345 000

c percentage change = $\dfrac{40\,000}{345\,000} \times 100$

= 11.594% = 11.6% (to 1 d.p.)

④ actual change = 352 − 324 = 28

original value = 324 tonnes

percentage increase = $\dfrac{28}{324} \times 100 = 8.642\%$

= 8.6% (to 1 d.p.)

Page 46

① **a** Measure the length of the scale provided for 1 μm and use this to estimate the actual length of the bacterium.

b image = 12 mm = 12 000 μm

actual length = 1 μm

magnification = $\dfrac{12\,000}{1} = \times 12\,000$

② **a** length of time for growth = 2017 − 1832 = 185 years

b You cannot have 0.108 108 of a person / they have not rounded to a sensible degree of accuracy.

Page 47

Exam-style question

1 **(a)** 10 cm **(1)**

(b) length at 120 hours = 10 cm, length at 150 hours = 17 cm, growth = 7 cm

rate of growth = 7 cm in 30 hours = $\dfrac{7}{30}$ **(1)**

= 0.233 333 = 0.23 cm/h (to 2 d.p.) **(1)**

(c) length at 120 hours = 10 cm, length at 180 hours = 24 cm, actual change = 14 cm **(1)**

percentage increase = $\dfrac{14}{10} \times 100$ **(1)**

= 140% **(1)**

Page 48

Exam-style question

1 **(a)** length of guard cell on image = 8 mm,

magnification = $\dfrac{8}{0.04}$ **(1)**

= ×200 **(1)**

(b) Rate of photosynthesis = $\dfrac{2.4}{8}$ **(1)**

= 0.3 cm³/h **(1)**

(c) actual change = 7.2 − 2.4 = 4.8

original value = 2.4 **(1)**

percentage increase = $\dfrac{4.8}{2.4} \times 100$ **(1)**

= 200% **(1)**

Unit 7

Page 50

① **a** Explain

b B

c so they move more quickly and collide more often

② **a** Describe the similarities and / or differences between things.

b Any three from: better adapted; more likely to survive; more likely to have the good adaptations; much quicker process as the non-adapted individuals do not breed.

Page 51

① **a** Describe

b Explain

c Draw

d Calculate

② **a** Explain

b coronary heart disease

c how being obese and smoking cigarettes increases

d smoke damages the artery wall; high blood pressure can damage the artery wall; fats build up in the artery

③ **a** Describe

b enzyme

c test a range of tissues for catalase activity

d decomposition of hydrogen peroxide to water and oxygen gas; gas can be collected by displacing water in an upturned test tube

Page 52

① Explain

② pH and temperature

③ **a** The active site is denatured by high temperature

At low temperatures enzyme activity is low

As temperature rises activity increases

This is because the enzyme molecules have more kinetic energy and collide more often

b At very high or low pH most enzymes are inactive

Extremes of pH will alter the shape of the active site

Enzymes work best at a particular pH called the optimum pH

④ **a** The active site is denatured by high temperature (4)

At low temperatures enzyme activity is low (1)

As temperature rises activity increases (2)

This is because the enzyme molecules have more kinetic energy and collide more often (3)

b At very high or low pH most enzymes are inactive (2)

Extremes of pH will alter the shape of the active site (3)

Enzymes work best at a particular pH called the optimum pH (1)

Page 53

① Make something clear, or state the reasons for something happening

② **a** C, D, E, F, G

b C = 2, D = 1, E = 5, F = 4, G = 3

Page 54

① Yes

② The coolness stops the microbes growing but also keeps the meat fresh without affecting the taste.

③ Yes

(4) No: the response does not cover the possible use of bleach.

(5) Yes it is logical. However, it could be improved by writing shorter paragraphs on each method or numbering the statements.

Page 55

(1) Evaluate

(2) Coronary heart disease

(3)

Treatment	Benefit	Risk
Drugs such as statins	Reduce blood cholesterol and deposition	Some side effects possible
Surgical – stents fitted	Not invasive surgery, holds the arteries open	Risk of infection from surgery, need to take anti-clotting drugs
Heart transplant	Improved health	Invasive surgery, risk of infection, finding a donor can be hard

(4) Put the benefits and risks of each treatment together.

(5) Sample answer

CHD can be treated by taking drugs such as statins, which help to reduce blood cholesterol levels. This reduces the risk of fat building up in the arteries and is relatively cheap. However, these medicines may cause side-effects, such as allergies or unexpected reactions in the cells.

If the arteries have been narrowed, this can cause conditions such as angina. In these cases, a stent can be fitted. This is a small mesh tube that holds the artery open. It is fitted via a small incision in the groin. A stent gives immediate relief and there is little recovery needed after the operation. However, there is always a risk of infection or blood clots forming. The patient will need to take anti-clotting drugs.

If the heart actually fails, a heart transplant will be needed. This could restore an active lifestyle but there are risks associated with open chest surgery, such as infection, and rejection is possible. The main difficulty is finding a suitable donor.

Page 56

Exam-style question

1 (a) Sample answer

Divide food into four parts. Crushing the food will help it to dissolve.

First sample: Dissolve the sample in water and add Benedict's reagent, then heat. A change in colour from blue to yellow / green / red shows sugars are present. Wear goggles while heating.

Second sample: Dissolve the sample in water and add iodine. A colour change from yellow-brown to blue-black shows starch is present.

Third sample: Dissolve the sample in water and add biuret reagent. A colour change from blue to purple shows protein present.

Fourth sample: Dissolve the sample in alcohol, filter, and add water to the clear filtrate. A change from clear to cloudy shows fat is present. Keep alcohol away from flame.

Chemistry

Unit 1

Page 58

(1)

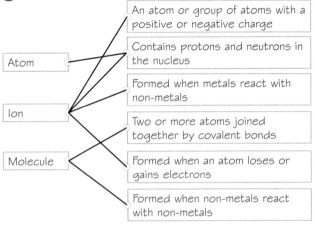

(2) Magnesium is a **metal and oxygen** is a non-metal. **Magnesium** atoms will react with oxygen **atoms** to form **magnesium** ions and oxide ions.

(3) (a) Sodium is a metal and chlorine is a non-metal. Atoms of sodium react with atoms of chlorine to form sodium ions and chloride ions.

(b) Carbon is a non-metal and oxygen is a non-metal. They react together to form a molecule of carbon dioxide. The atoms in the molecule are joined by sharing electrons, in a covalent bond.

Page 59

(1) (a)

Element	Electronic configuration		Correction
lithium ($Z = 3$)	2.1	✓	
fluorine ($Z = 9$)	2.6		2.7
aluminium ($Z = 13$)	2.8.3	✓	
calcium ($Z = 20$)	2.8.8		2.8.8.2

(b) Fluorine is a non-metal atom with 7 electrons in its outer shell. It gains one electron to achieve a full outer shell of electrons, forming a negatively charged ion.

(2)

	Number of protons (and their charge)	Number of electrons (and their charge)	Overall charge	Symbol
Chlorine atom ($Z = 17$)	17 (+17)	17 (−17)	0	Cl
Chloride ion	17 (+17)	18 (−18)	−1	Cl⁻
Magnesium atom ($Z = 12$)	12 (+12)	12 (−12)	0	Mg
Magnesium ion	12 (+12)	10 (−10)	+2	Mg²⁺

(3) (a) A potassium atom has an electronic configuration of 2.8.8.1. When a potassium atom reacts, it loses one electron from its outer shell, to form a potassium ion $(2.8.8)^+$. The ion has 19 protons and only 18 electrons, so it has a +1 charge.

(b) K^+, $(2.8.8)^+$

Page 60

① **a** Chlorine

2.8.7

b Chloride ion

[2.8.8]⁻

②

Lithium atom 2.1   Fluorine atom 2.7   →   Lithium ion [2]⁺   Fluorine ion [2.8]⁻

Page 61

Exam-style question

① A, C

② **a** Compounds W and Y

b Both of the compounds W and Y conduct electricity when they are in the molten state, as their ions are free to move and carry the current. However, compounds W and Y do not conduct electricity when they are solid. This is because their ions cannot move around in the fixed lattice structure.

Page 62

① **a** K⁺

b The student has selected an element which is not an ion but which would form a cation (positively charged ion).

② **a** B

b Student B has explained that the atoms have lost and gained electrons.

Student B has stated how many electrons have been lost from the magnesium atom and gained by the oxygen atom ("two electrons are transferred") to form the ions.

Page 63

① 'Explain' means that you must say how or why something happens.

② **a** Yes, it is formed from magnesium which is a metal and chlorine which is a non-metal.

b Magnesium gains electrons, oxygen loses electrons.

c Ionic compound.

d Strong electrostatic forces of attraction – ionic bonds.

e A giant lattice structure.

③ An explanation that combines identification – knowledge (1 mark) and reasoning/justification – understanding (2 marks):

very strong bonds/ionically bonded **(1)**

between 2⁺ cations and 2⁻ anions **(1)**

so requires lot of energy to separate magnesium and oxide ions to melt the solid **(1)**

Page 64

1 Sodium chloride contains sodium ions and chloride ions, Na⁺ and Cl⁻, **(1)** which are held together by strong ionic bonds between the ions. **(1)** Sodium chloride has a giant lattice structure therefore it has a high melting point as a lot of energy is needed to separate the ions. **(1)** When molten or in aqueous solution the ions in sodium chloride are free to move, so it conducts electricity. **(1)**

Unit 2

Page 66

① **a** sulfuric acid

b copper oxide

c copper sulfate

② **a** chloride is wrong; magnesium sulfate

b nitrate is wrong; copper chloride

c potassium is wrong; sodium nitrate

Page 67

① **a** No

b hydrochloric acid

c acid: hydrochloric acid

base: magnesium oxide/magnesium carbonate/magnesium hydroxide

d No

② **b** reactants: zinc oxide + nitric acid

method: add excess of the insoluble base to warm acid, filter off excess base, evaporate filtrate to remove some of the water, leave until crystals form

c reactants: sodium hydroxide + sulfuric acid

method: soluble base so use titration, use same volumes to react, then evaporate filtrate to remove some of the water, leave until crystals form

Page 68

① **a** zinc oxide + hydrochloric acid ⟶ zinc chloride + water

or zinc hydroxide + hydrochloric acid ⟶ zinc chloride + water

or zinc carbonate + hydrochloric acid ⟶ zinc chloride + carbon dioxide + water

b B, A, D, C, E

c Water bath: used to heat the acid, to make sure the reaction is complete, when the acid reacts with the base.

Evaporating basin: used so the filtrate can be heated safely, to remove some of the water, until crystals start to form.

d Evaporation and Filtration

Page 69

① A No; water bath

B No; look for an excess of the oxide, with some solid left in the solution

No; filtration

C No; use an evaporating dish, on top of a water bath

No; Until the solution is gone/only solid is left

② An explanation that combines identification of an improvement to the procedure and a reason that must be linked to the improvement:

• Add an excess of magnesium oxide to react with all of the acid, the maximum amount of magnesium chloride will be formed.

- Filter off the excess magnesium oxide, to remove any excess, which would be an impurity.
- Evaporate off some of the water and then leave for crystals to form, so that no crystals are lost by spitting/excessive heating.
- Place the magnesium chloride in a warm oven/warm place/dry with filter paper so the magnesium chloride crystals are dry.

Page 70

(1) See answer to Q2.

(2) Possible answers include:

Errors	Corrections
1 Sulfuric acid is suggested to be used to make magnesium nitrate.	Nitric acid (not sulfuric acid) should be used to make magnesium nitrate.
2 The equation is incorrect.	The correct equation is: $MgO(s) + 2HNO_3(aq) \rightarrow Mg(NO_3)_2(aq) + H_2O(l)$
3 Using a beaker to measure out the $25\,cm^3$ of acid.	Use a measuring cylinder to measure out a specific volume of acid.
4 Heating the acid using a Bunsen burner.	Use a water bath to heat the acid, as it is a safer technique.
5 Adding the solution to a beaker for the evaporation step.	Transfer the magnesium nitrate solution to an evaporating basin and place over a beaker of water, heated with a Bunsen burner, to evaporate off some of the water.

Page 71

(1) Some notes to help you check your answer:
- suitable acid: hydrochloric acid
- suitable base: copper oxide/copper carbonate
- equation for reaction:
  either $CuO + 2HCl \rightarrow CuCl_2 + H_2O$
  or $CuCO_3 + 2HCl \rightarrow CuCl_2 + H_2O + CO_2$
- **either** add solid copper compound to warmed acid until excess solid remains (oxide)
  or add solid a little at a time until no more bubbles (carbonate)
- filter off the excess solid, pour remaining solution into an evaporating basin
- heat solution / leave the water to evaporate until pure salt crystals form and then dry salt crystals with absorbent paper/leave to dry

(2) Improvements: identify two suitable improvements after comparing your answer to the checklist.

Page 72

Exam-style question

1 $MgCO_3(s) + H_2SO_4(aq) \rightarrow MgSO_4(aq) + H_2O(l) + CO_2(g)$ **(2)**
(marks are given for correct chemical formulae and for the equation being balanced)

2 Some notes to help you check your answer:
- suitable acid: nitric acid
- suitable base: zinc oxide / zinc carbonate
- equation for reaction:
  either $ZnO + 2HNO \rightarrow Zn(NO_3)_2 + H_2O$
  or $ZnCO_3 + 2HNO_3 \rightarrow Zn(NO_3)_2 + H_2O + CO_2$
  AO3 (3 marks)
- **either** add solid to warmed acid until excess solid remains (oxide)

or add solid a little at a time until no more bubbles (carbonate)
- filter off the excess solid, pour remaining solution into an evaporating basin
- heat solution / leave the water to evaporate until pure salt crystals form and then dry salt crystals with absorbent paper/leave to dry

Unit 3
Page 74

(1) decomposed, electrolysis, conduct, move

(2) a K^+, Mg^{2+}
    b F^-, Cl^-, SO_4^{2-}

(3) Electrolyte – An ionic compound which conducts electricity when molten or dissolved in water
Electrolysis – A process in which electrical energy, from a direct current, decomposes electrolytes
Decomposition – To break down a compound into simpler compounds or into elements

Page 75

(1)

	Product at the cathode	Product at the anode
lead bromide	lead	bromine
potassium iodide	potassium	iodine
copper chloride	copper	chlorine

(2) a potassium metal / $K(l)$
    b bromine liquid / $Br_2(l)$

(3) a molten
    b molten
    c Solid sodium chloride has an ordered lattice structure where the ions cannot move. Therefore the solid does not conduct electricity and cannot be electrolysed. In molten sodium chloride, the ionic bonds holding the ions together have been broken by heating. This allows the ions to move freely and conduct electricity. Molten sodium chloride can be electrolysed as the ions are free to move.

Page 76

(1)

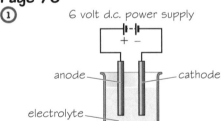

6 volt d.c. power supply

anode — cathode

electrolyte

(2) a reduction
    b oxidation

(3) a at the cathode
    b at the anode
    c At the cathode, positive ions gain electrons to form atoms. Reduction is the gain of electrons.
    At the anode, negative ions lose electrons to form atoms. Oxidation is the loss of electrons.

Page 77

(1) a potassium ions (K^+), chloride ions (Cl^-)
    b (i) chloride ions (Cl^-)
       (ii) potassium ions (K^+)
    c potassium and chlorine are formed.

(2) sodium ions (Na^+), iodide ions (I^-), hydrogen ions (H^+), hydroxide ions (OH^-)

③ a Copper forms at the cathode because it is less reactive than hydrogen: $Cu^{2+} + 2e^- \rightarrow Cu$

b Oxygen gas forms because sulfate ions are polyatomic: $4OH^- \rightarrow 2H_2O + O_2 + 4e^-$

④ a $Cl^-(aq)$, $H^+(aq)$, $K^+(aq)$, $OH^-(aq)$

b $H_2(g)$, $Cl_2(g)$

Page 78

① a The sample student answer would gain 1 mark. They have stated that the hydrogen and copper ions are attracted to the cathode, while hydroxide and sulfate ions are attracted to the anode. However, they have not included the other three points from the mark scheme.

b Improvements may include:
o State the ions are attracted to the oppositely charged electrode.
o Explain what happens to the ions, in terms of electrons. State which ions lose electrons and which ions gain electrons.
o State what is formed at each electrode, e.g. a copper atom/an oxygen molecule.

② Positive ions are attracted to the negatively charged electrode, the cathode; and negatively charged ions are attracted to the positively charged electrode, the anode (1). Copper sulfate solution contains copper ions (Cu2+) and hydrogen ions (H+) which are attracted to the cathode, and sulfate ions (SO42-) and hydroxide ions (OH-) which are attracted to the anode (1). A copper ion, Cu2+, will accept 2 electrons to form a copper atom, Cu (1). Four hydroxide ions, OH-, will lose 4 electrons to form an oxygen molecule, O2 (1).

Page 79

Exam-style question

① a An electrolyte is an ionic compound that conducts electricity (1) when molten or dissolved in water. (1)

b i Solution – Are the ions free to move? The solute is dissolved in water. Some water is ionised.

Hydrogen – Why is sodium not a product? What happens to the ions?

ii Hydrogen ions (H+) and sodium (Na+) ions are attracted to cathode, hydroxide (OH−) ions and chloride (Cl−) ions are attracted to anode (1) because the ions are attracted to the oppositely charged electrode. (1) Two hydrogen ions (2H+) accept two electrons to form a hydrogen molecule, $H_2(g)$. (1) Two chloride ions (2Cl−) lose two electrons to form a chlorine molecule, $Cl_2(g)$. (1)

Page 80

1 (a) F and H are electrolytes (1) because their solutions conduct electricity and are decomposed in the process. (1)

(b) Hydrogen (H+) ions and potassium (K+) ions are attracted to cathode, hydroxide (OH−) ions and sulfate (SO4²−) ions are attracted to anode, (1) because ions are attracted to the oppositely charged electrode. (1)

Two hydrogen ions / 2H+(aq) accept two electrons to form hydrogen molecule / $H_2(g)$ (1).

Four hydroxide ions / 4OH−(aq) lose four electrons to form oxygen molecule / $O_2(g)$ (1)

Unit 4
page 82

① a 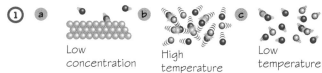 b c

Low concentration / High temperature / Low temperature

② If particles collide and they do not have the energy needed to react (the activation energy), then they will not react to form products.

③ The lighted splint provides the methane gas particles with the activation energy required to start the reaction with oxygen in the air, in a combustion reaction.

page 83

① A

② Increasing the concentration of the solution increases the rate of reaction. This is because there are more reacting particles in the same volume of solution, so the frequency of collisions increases, increasing the rate of reaction.

page 84

① a Independent variable: temperature of the hydrochloric acid.

Dependent variable: time taken for the magnesium to react and disappear.

b Independent variable: surface area of marble chips.

Dependent variable: volume of gas produced (carbon dioxide).

② a Time for the cross to disappear, due to the sulfur precipitate.

b The temperature.

c One of: concentration of hydrochloric acid, concentration of sodium thiosulfate solution, size of beaker/flask, depth of liquid in beaker/flask.

d As the temperature increases, the time for the cross to disappear decreases, so the rate of reaction increases with increasing temperature.

Page 85

① $\text{rate} = \dfrac{\text{volume of gas produced}}{\text{time}} = \dfrac{4.5}{5.0} = 0.9 \text{ cm}^3/\text{s}$

② a

(i) All points plotted correctly, with a line of best fit drawn through the points.

(ii) The line of best fit drawn will be above the first line plotted and steeper, as the concentration of acid is higher.

b $2.1 \text{ cm}^3/\text{s}$

Page 86

1. The key is missing from the graph, to identify which is the curve for large pieces and which is the curve for small pieces.

   Units are also missing from the labels on the axes. The y-axis shows the volume, so the unit is cm^3. The x-axis shows the time, so the unit will probably be s, but could be min.

   The title for the graph is needed "A graph to show the volume of gas produced against time, for large and small pieces of calcium carbonate."

2. By including ideas about particles colliding.

   Improved answer: For the smaller sized pieces, there is more surface area for collisions to occur on, so more particles are available for the acid to collide with, so the frequency of collisions increases and the rate of reaction increases.

Page 87

Exam-style question

1. a. The reaction with the fastest rate is the higher concentration curve. **(1)**

   This is because the graph is steeper and levels off more quickly. **(1)**

   b. As the concentration of acid increases, the volume of gas produced per second increases **(1)**, so the rate of reaction increases **(1)**.

   c. The rate of reaction increases as the temperature increases because the reacting particles speed up and have more energy **(1)**. They therefore collide more frequently **(1)** and more particles have enough energy (activation energy) to react when they collide **(1)**.

Page 88

Exam-style question

1. The sulfur produced in the reaction is a yellow precipitate, which means it is a solid product **(1)**. The reaction takes place in a flask. The flask is placed on top of a piece of paper with a cross on it. The flask is observed from above. The reaction is timed until enough sulfur is produced that the cross disappears **(1)**.

2. $rate = \dfrac{volume\ of\ gas\ produced}{time} = \dfrac{15}{10} = 1.5\ cm^3/s$ **(2)**

Unit 5

Page 90

1. a. A_r oxygen = 16.0
   b. A_r calcium = 40.0
   c. A_r magnesium = 24.0
2. 8
3. a. B
   b. Answer B shows the chemical symbol for an isotope of chlorine, known as chlorine-37.

      They both have the same atomic number of 17, so they are the same element (chlorine). However, they have different mass numbers (35 and 37), which shows they have a different number of neutrons. Isotopes have the same atomic number but a different mass number, so they have the same number of protons but a different number of neutrons.
4. a. relative formula mass = $(2 \times 1) + (1 \times 16) = 18$
5. a. 44
   b. 98

Page 91

1. Relative formula mass of iron oxide
   $= (2 \times A_r\ of\ Fe) + (3 \times A_r\ of\ oxygen)$
   $= (2 \times 56) + (3 \times 16)$
   $= 112 + 48 = \underline{160}$

2. Relative formula mass of calcium hydroxide
   $= Ar\ of\ Ca + 2 \times (Ar\ O + Ar\ H)$
   $= 40 + 2(1 + 16)$
   $= 40 + 34 = \underline{74}$

Page 92

1. a.

Elements	Sodium, Na	Oxygen, O
Mass of each element (g)	0.69	0.24
Divide the mass of each element by the relative atomic mass (A_r) for that element	$\dfrac{0.69}{23} = 0.03$	$\dfrac{0.24}{16} = 0.02$
Divide the answers by the smallest number to find the simplest whole number ratio	$\dfrac{0.03}{0.015} = 2$	$\dfrac{0.02}{0.02} = 1$

   b. Ratio is $2 : 1$ so Na_2O

2. a.

Elements	C	O
Mass of each element (g)	0.24	0.64
Divide the mass by the relative atomic mass (A_r)	$\dfrac{0.24}{12} = 0.02$	$\dfrac{0.64}{16} = 0.04$
Divide the answers by the smallest number	$\dfrac{0.02}{0.02} = 1$	$\dfrac{0.04}{0.02} = 2$

   b. Ratio is $1 : 2$ so CO_2

3.

Elements	Fe	Cl
Mass of each element (g)	11.2	14.2
Divide the mass by the relative atomic mass (A_r)	$\dfrac{11.2}{56.0} = 0.2$	$\dfrac{14.2}{35.5} = 0.4$
Divide the answers by the smallest number	$\dfrac{0.2}{0.2} = 1$	$\dfrac{0.4}{0.2} = 2$
Empirical formula	Ratio is $1 : 2$ $FeCl_2$	

Page 93

1. a. $(65 \times 1) + (16 \times 1) = 81$
   b. 2Zn gives 2ZnO, so 2 x 65 g of Zn gives 2 x 81 of ZnO. This means that 130g of Zn gives 162g of ZnO.
   c.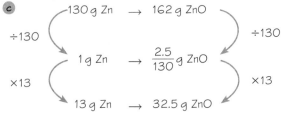
   d. 81

2. a. relative atomic mass of Mg = 24
      relative atomic mass of H2 = 2
   b. $1\ Mg \rightarrow 1\ H_2$, so $1 \times 24\ g\ Mg \rightarrow 1 \times 2\ g\ H_2$
   c. $24\ g\ Mg \rightarrow 2\ g\ H_2$
      $1\ g\ Mg \rightarrow \dfrac{2}{24}\ g\ H_2$
   d. $7.2\ g\ Mg \rightarrow 0.6\ g\ H_2$

Page 94

1. a All steps are included, to calculate the mass of water produced.

   Working out is shown for most of the steps (although relative formula mass calculations are not shown fully).

   b The answer is incorrect, as the student has calculated the M_r of water as $2H_2O$. It should be just H_2O. The correct answer is 7.2 g of water produced.

   Units are missing from the answer. The units should be g, as it is a mass.

Page 95

Exam-style question

1. a Relative formula mass of Na_2CO_3

   $= (2 \times A_r\ Na) + A_r\ C + (3 \times A_r\ O)$

   $= (2 \times 23) + 12 + (3 \times 16)$

   $= 106$ **(1)**

   b

$Na_2CO_3(s) + 2HCl(aq) \rightarrow 2NaCl(aq) + H_2O(l) + CO_2(g)$
?g   24.0 g
Relative atomic mass of NaCl is given in part (a): 58.5
Relative atomic mass of Na_2CO_3 was calculated in part (a): 106
1 Na_2CO_3 makes 2 NaCl
So 1×106 g of Na_2CO_3 makes 2×58.5 g of NaCl
So 106 g of Na_2CO_3 makes 117 g of NaCl

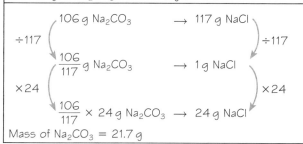

Mass of Na_2CO_3 = 21.7 g

2.

Elements	Cu	O
Mass of each element (g)	1.27	0.32
Divide the mass by the relative atomic mass (A_r)	$\dfrac{1.27}{63.5} = 0.02$	$\dfrac{0.32}{16} = 0.02$
Divide the answers by the smallest number	$\dfrac{0.02}{0.02} = 1$	$\dfrac{0.02}{0.02} = 1$
Empirical formula	\multicolumn{2}{c}{Ratio is 1 : 1}
	\multicolumn{2}{c}{CuO}

Page 96

Exam-style question

1.

Elements	Cu	Cl
Mass of each element (g)	15.9	17.7
Divide the mass by the relative atomic mass (A_r)	$\dfrac{15.9}{63.5} = 0.25$	$\dfrac{17.7}{35.5} = 0.50$
Divide the answers by the smallest number	$\dfrac{0.25}{0.25} = 1$	$\dfrac{0.50}{0.25} = 2$
Empirical formula	\multicolumn{2}{c}{Ratio is 1 : 2}
	\multicolumn{2}{c}{$CuCl_2$}

2.

$CaO(s) + 2HCl(aq) \rightarrow CaCl_2(aq) + H_2O\ (l)$
2.8 g   ? g
Relative atomic mass of CaO A_r Ca + A_r O $= 40.0 + 16.0 = 56.0$
Relative formula mass of $CaCl_2 = A_r$ Ca + $(2 \times A_r$ Cl) $= 40 + (2 \times 35.5) = 40 + 71 = 111$
1 CaO makes 1 $CaCl_2$ So 1×56 g of CaO makes 1×111 g of $CaCl_2$

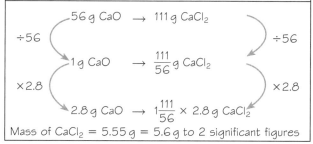

Mass of $CaCl_2 = 5.55$ g $= 5.6$ g to 2 significant figures

Unit 6

Page 98

1. a CO   b Cl_2 c C_2H_6
2. a zinc oxide
   b potassium bromide
3. C_3H_8

Page 99

1. a symbols: Na and O
   b ions: Na^+ and O^{2-}
   c balance charges: $(+1) + (+1) + (-2) = 0$
   d chemical formula: $2 \times Na, 1 \times O = Na_2O$
2. symbols: Ca and OH
   ions: Ca^{2+} and OH^-
   balance charges $(+2) + (-1) + (-1) = 0$
   chemical formula: $1 \times Ca, 2 \times OH = Ca(OH)_2$

Page 100

1. a magnesium, oxygen
   b 1
   c There is only one product, which is magnesium oxide. This is a compound formed from the elements magnesium and oxygen.
2. zinc oxide + sulfuric acid $\rightarrow$ zinc sulfate + water
3. a sodium chloride
   b sodium hydroxide + hydrochloric acid $\rightarrow$ sodium chloride + water

Page 101

1. $\underline{2}Zn(s) + O_2(g) \rightarrow \underline{2}ZnO(s)$
2. $\underline{2}K(s) + \underline{2}H_2O(l) \rightarrow \underline{2}KOH(aq) + H_2(g)$

	Number of atoms on reactants side		Number of atoms on products side	
	Original equation	Balanced equation	Original equation	Balanced equation
potassium, K	1	2	1	2
oxygen, O	1	2	1	2
hydrogen, H	2	4	3	4 [2 in 2KOH and 2 in H_2]

Page 102

(1) The word 'dilute' is not needed in the word equation, so leave it out.

The word 'salt' is not needed in the word equation, so leave it out.

(2)

Formula	Correct? ✓ / ✗	Correction
Reactants: $Na_2CO_3 + HCl$	✓	
Products: $NaCl + H_2O + Co_2$	✗	Co_2 should be written as CO_2 CO_2 is the formula for carbon dioxide, but Co is the symbol for cobalt.
Balancing: $2Na_2CO_3 + 2HCl \rightarrow$ $2\ NaCl + H_2O + 3Co_2$	✓ HCl ✓ NaCl ✗ $2Na_2CO_3$ ✗ $3Co_2$	No balancing number is required for Na_2CO_3 or CO_2.

c The correct balanced equation is $Na_2CO_3(s)$ + $2HCl(aq) \rightarrow 2NaCl(aq) + H_2O(l) + CO_2(g)$

Page 103

Exam-style question

(1) a sodium hydroxide + sulfuric acid $\rightarrow$ sodium sulfate + water **(2)**

b $\underline{2}NaOH(aq) + H_2SO_4(aq) \rightarrow Na_2SO_4(aq) +$ $\underline{2}H_2O(l)$ **(2)**

	Number of atoms on reactants side		Number of atoms on products side	
	Original equation	Balanced equation	Original equation	Balanced equation
sodium, Na	1	2	2	2
oxygen, O	5	6	5	6
hydrogen, H	3	4	2	4
sulfur, S	1	1	1	1

(2) $2Na(s) + 2H_2O(l) \rightarrow 2NaOH(aq) + H_2(g)$ **(3)**

Page 104

Exam-style question

1 **(a)** (s) is the state symbol, as an insoluble precipitate is a solid. **(1)**

(b) calcium hydroxide + carbon dioxide $\rightarrow$ calcium carbonate + water **(1)**

(c) $Ca(OH)_2(aq) + CO_2(g) \rightarrow CaCO_3(s) + H_2O(l)$ **(3)**

Unit 7

Page 106

(1) Answers may refer to:

Highlighting key words or information in the question.

Practising answering extended writing questions and then using mark scheme to mark answers.

Peer assessing answers from other students.

(2) – (4) Student's own responses.

Page 107

(1) a Explain: I need to say why oil companies use cracking.

b Cracking: breaking down large hydrocarbon molecules into smaller, more useful ones.

c Explain why it is necessary for oil companies to use cracking on some fractions obtained from crude oil.

d Percentage obtained and percentage required. More petrol is needed than is obtained. More kerosene is obtained than is needed (so some kerosene is not needed).

Number of carbon atoms in molecules. Cracking kerosene molecules will make shorter molecules, which may be in the petrol fraction.

e "Some fractions": I need to decide which fraction is used for cracking.

(2) The question is asking me to explain what cracking is, what the data tells me about the amounts of each fraction available and the amounts needed by customers. I need to use some data from the table in my answer and say why oil companies use cracking, which fraction is used for cracking and what this produces.

Page 108

(1) Describe

(2) You should have identified key information such as properties, variables and clues towards an experiment: room temperature, decomposes slowly, hydrogen peroxide forms water and oxygen, a catalyst increases rate of reaction, the mass of a catalyst is unchanged, progress of a reaction can be followed measuring the volume of a gas (oxygen) given off.

(3) Make notes such as the following:

Variables to control are the concentration and volume of hydrogen peroxide solution.

Chemicals to be used are hydrogen peroxide solution and the manganese(IV) oxide solid...

To measure the rate of reaction - possibly the time taken for an amount of gas to be produced..

Apparatus: to measure the mass of solid manganese(IV) oxide, use a balance; to measure the volume of gas, use a measuring cylinder over water or a gas syringe…

Do experiment with and without the manganese(IV) oxide.

(4) Oxygen gas is produced. Measure the volume of gas produced using a gas syringe or a measuring cylinder over water.

(5) a Measure a volume of hydrogen peroxide solution ($25\ cm^3$) and keep this the same for all experiments. Collect the gas produced using a measuring cylinder over water, without a catalyst. Time the reaction for a fixed amount of gas to be produced. Repeat the experiment, using 1 g of manganese(IV) oxide, keep everything else the same. If the manganese(IV) oxide increases the rate, then the time taken to collect a fixed volume of gas will be less, so it is acting as a catalyst.

b Use a balance to measure 1 g of solid manganese(IV) oxide at the start of the experiment. At the end, filter off the solid, wash and dry and measure the mass again. If the mass is unchanged and the rate has increased, then the manganese(IV) oxide is acting as a catalyst.

Page 109

(1) A and C

(2) A and C

(3) Sample answer

The variable being changed is the use of a catalyst. First carry out the reaction without the catalyst, then repeat the experiment with the catalyst. Variables being controlled are the volume of hydrogen peroxide solution, the fixed volume of gas being produced, the temperature of the solutions. The time taken for a fixed volume of gas to be produced will give a measure of the rate of reaction.

To measure the volume of oxygen gas produced, use a measuring cylinder over water or a gas syringe. To measure the mass of catalyst, use a balance. To measure the time taken to produce a fixed volume of gas, use a stop clock.

Measure a volume of hydrogen peroxide (e.g. 20 cm³) and collect the gas produced using a measuring cylinder over water, without a catalyst. Time the reaction to produce a fixed amount of gas. Repeat the experiment keeping everything the same, adding manganese(IV) oxide (e.g. 1 g). Filter off the catalyst, wash and dry then measure the mass at the end.

If the time for the fixed volume of gas to be produced is lower using the manganese(IV) oxide then the reaction is faster and it shows that manganese(IV) oxide is acting as a catalyst.

If the mass of the manganese(IV) oxide is the same after the reaction as before, then the mass is unchanged and the manganese(IV) oxide is acting as a catalyst.

Page 110

1 a "Cracking is a process which breaks down larger hydrocarbon molecules into smaller, more useful ones. The smaller molecules are more useful, as fuels, e.g. petrol."

b "Oil companies use cracking so they can meet the demands of customers for the amount of petrol required and they do not have too much kerosene left over."

2 a No

b The student has not included any of the data provided for kerosene or petrol. Only 8% of kerosene is required; however, 13% is produced. This is compared with petrol, where 26% is required and only 10% is produced.

Therefore, kerosene will be used for cracking, as there is a surplus. Kerosene contains molecules with more carbon atoms in than petrol, so they can be broken down to produce smaller molecules including petrol. This enables the demand for petrol to be met.

Page 111

1, 2 Sample answer

The reactivity increases from lithium to sodium to potassium, as you go down the group.

All of the metals produce hydrogen gas and a solution of the metal hydroxide.

e.g. $2Li(s) + 2H_2O(l) \rightarrow 2LiOH(aq) + H_2(g)$

The metals effervesce and float on the water, moving across the water surface. The reactions become more vigorous from lithium to potassium. Sodium and potassium melt and potassium burns with a lilac flame.

Group 1 metals react by losing one electron from the outer shell, to form a positive ion. The electronic configurations for the group 1 metals are:

Lithium (Li) 2.1

Sodium (Na) 2.8.1

Potassium (K) 2.8.8.1

The electron in the outer shell is lost more easily as you go down the group, from lithium to potassium, because the electron in the outer shell is further from the nucleus. The force of attraction from the positive nucleus to the negative electron is reduced going down the group, therefore the electron is lost more easily and the ion is formed more easily. This means that the reactivity increases, due to the increasing number of shells, going down the group from lithium to potassium.

Page 112

1 Student's own answer.

2 Student's own answer.

Physics
Unit 1
Page 114

1

Energy store	Stored in...
chemical energy	atoms
elastic potential or strain energy	food, fuel and batteries
gravitational potential energy	hot objects
kinetic energy	moving objects
nuclear or atomic energy	objects in high positions
thermal energy	stretched, squashed or twisted materials

2 a i friction
   ii electricity
   iii heat

b electricity, sound, thermal

Page 115

1 energy stored in the battery as chemical energy
energy transferred by electricity
energy stored as kinetic energy

2 a energy stored as strain energy in the spring
energy transferred by forces
energy stored as kinetic energy

b energy stored in the twig as gravitational potential energy
transferred by forces (gravity)
energy stored as kinetic energy

Page 116

1 a kinetic, sound, thermal

b

	useful energy store(s)	wasted energy store(s)
electric toothbrush	kinetic	thermal sound
electric hairdryer	kinetic thermal	sound

2 a i kinetic
   ii GPE and kinetic (either order)

b The energy has been dissipated to the ground and surrounding air.

c ii has been dissipated to the ground and surrounding air as heat.

Page 117

1 a $\text{efficiency} = \dfrac{\text{useful energy transferred}}{\text{total energy supplied}}$

b i car   ii 200 J   iii 50 J

c efficiency $= \dfrac{50\,J}{200\,J} = 0.25\,J$

Page 118

① **a** Describes the transfers rather than just stating the stores

  b Describes the transfers for both up and down

② Describes

③ The energy is transferred to thermal energy ✓ which is used to heat up the water ✓ and some is lost to the surroundings ✓.

④ **a** 100 J

  b 1000 J

  c values for efficiency should be between 0 and 1

  d Correct response:

efficiency $= \dfrac{\text{useful energy transferred by the device}}{\text{total energy supplied to the device}}$

$= \dfrac{100\,J}{1000}\,J$

$= 0.1$

Page 119

Exam-style question

① **a** Chemical energy is transferred (by electricity) to kinetic energy. **(1)**

  b i Energy is wasted as thermal energy or sound energy **(1)**

    ii This energy is dissipated/lost to the surroundings e.g. the vacuum cleaner and the air. **(1)**

  c

efficiency $= \dfrac{\text{useful energy transferred by the device}}{\text{total energy supplied to the device}}$ **(1)**

useful energy 65 J

total energy supplied 100 J

$= \dfrac{65\,J}{100\,J}$ **(1)**

$= 0.65$ **(1)**

Page 120

Exam-style question

1 **a** Energy is transferred by electricity to light (or sound) energy. **(1)**

  b Energy is wasted as thermal energy **(1)** lost to the surroundings e.g. the TV and the air. **(1)**

2 useful energy transferred by the device = efficiency × total energy supplied to the device **(1)**

$= 0.2 \times 50\,J$ **(1)**

$= 10\,J$ **(1)**

Unit 2

Page 122

① **a** i C

    ii It is the longest arrow

  b i D and B

    ii A and C

② 2N

③ 5 N downwards.

④ speed $= \dfrac{\text{distance}}{\text{time}}$

Page 123

① i unbalanced

  ii to the left

  iii changes

  iv accelerates

② **a** Reaction force and weight force.

  b i No

    ii There is no movement

  c right, changes

Page 124

① **a** speed $= \dfrac{40}{10} = 4\,m/s$

  b steeper line means it is going faster

  c speed $= \dfrac{40}{4} = 10\,m/s$

Page 125

① 6 s × 5 m/s = 30 m

② Total = 10 m + 30 m = 40 m

Page 126

① A. The object travels at a constant velocity of 10 m/s for 150 s.

  B. The object accelerates from 10 m/s to 40 m/s in the next 100 s

  C. The object travels at constant velocity of 40 m/s for 50 s.

  D. The object decelerates from 40 m/s back down to 0 m/s over the next 50 s.

  b i The student has read the speed as 15 m/s not 10 m/s.

    ii Correct answer is 150 s × 10 m/s = 1500 m

Page 127

Exam-style question

1 a A **(1)**

  b The backward force is now bigger than the forward force so the horizontal forces are unbalanced. **(1)** There is a resultant force in the backwards direction. **(1)**

  c i A. The Segway travels at a constant speed for 2 minutes. **(1)**

    B. The Segway is stationary for 1 minute. **(1)**

    C. The Segway travels at a constant speed for 2 minutes, faster than during part A. **(1)**

    ii speed $= \dfrac{\text{distance}}{\text{time}}$ OR correct gradient lines drawn on graph **(1)**

    time is 2 minutes = 2 × 60 s = 120 s **(1)**

    speed = gradient $= \dfrac{200\,m}{120\,s}$ **(1)**

    $= 1.67\,m/s$ **(1)**

Page 128

Exam-style question

1 **a**

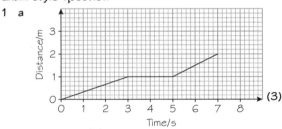

  (3)

  b speed $= \dfrac{\text{distance}}{\text{time}}$ (or show gradient lines on graph or state) **(1)**

    $= \dfrac{1\,m}{2\,s}$ (or object moves 1 m in 2 s) **(1)**

    $= 0.5\,m/s$ **(1)**

Unit 3

Page 130

1 Component   Symbol

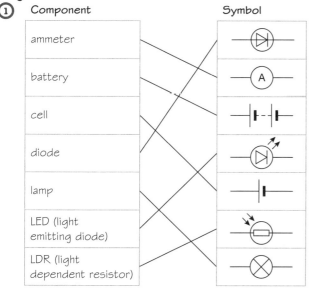

Component   Symbol

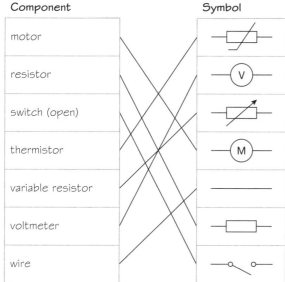

2 **a** $\text{current (A)} = \dfrac{\text{potential difference (V)}}{\text{resistance }(\Omega)}$

     b $\text{resistance }(\Omega) = \dfrac{\text{potential difference (V)}}{\text{current (A)}}$

3 A transformer changes the potential difference in a circuit while keeping the electrical power the same.

Page 131

1 **a** battery

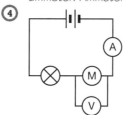

     b thermistor

     c variable resistor

     d diode

     e resistor

2 **a** amperes / amps

     b volts

3

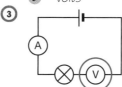

Voltmeter should be in parallel with lamp.

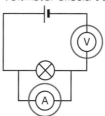

Voltmeter should be in parallel with lamp, and ammeter should be in series (voltmeter and ammeter are the wrong way around).

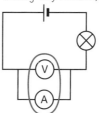

Voltmeter should be in parallel with lamp, not ammeter. Ammeter should be in series with lamp.

4

Page 132

1 lower

     higher

2 **a** current doubles

     b resistance stays the same

3 **a** more

     b less

Page 133

1 **a** Increases voltage

     b To reduce the current so less energy is lost as heat/efficiency is increased

2 **a** decreases voltage

     b Consumers in homes and workplaces use electricity at lower voltages.

3 Step-up transformer has more turns in the secondary coil than the primary.

Step-down transformer has more turns in the primary coil than the secondary.

Page 134

1 **a** answer A

        resistance = voltage × current this is the wrong equation

               = 6V × 0.6A correct values but wrong calculation

               = 3.6 Ω incorrect answer but has remembered units   0 marks

answer B

$$\text{resistance} = \frac{\text{voltage}}{\text{current}}$$ ✓ correct equation

$$= \frac{0.6A}{6V}$$ ✗ incorrect substitution of values

$$= 0.1$$ ✗ incorrect answer and also forgotten units 1 mark

b 3 mark answer:

$$\text{resistance} = \frac{\text{voltage}}{\text{current}}$$ ✓ correct equation

$$= \frac{6V}{0.6A}$$ ✓ correct equation

$$= 10\,\Omega$$ ✓ correct answer with unit 3 marks

(2)

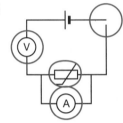

Voltmeter in series not parallel.
Thermistor symbol not variable resistor.
Ammeter is in parallel not series.
Gap in the circuit.

Page 135

Exam-style question

(1) **a**

Quantity	Measured using	Connected in
voltage	a voltmeter	parallel
current	an ammeter	series

b

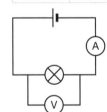

Correct symbol for voltmeter connected across the lamp. **(1)**

Correct symbol for ammeter in series with the lamp. **(1)**

Correct symbol for lamp and cell connected in series. **(1)**

Lose one mark for any gap in the circuit greater than 1 mm (except in the cell).

(2) $R = \frac{V}{I}$ **(1)**

(3) Step-up transformer increases voltage in a circuit **(1)**
Step-down transformer decreases voltage in a circuit **(1)**

Page 136

Exam-style question

1

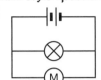

correct symbol for lamp **(1)**
correct symbol for motor **(1)**
cells, lamp and motor in parallel **(1)**
correct symbol for both cells **(1)**

2 **a** $I = \frac{V}{R}$ **(1)**

$$= \frac{12V}{3\Omega}$$ **(1)**

$$= 4\,A$$ **(1)**

b As the resistance increases the current will decrease. **(1)**

Unit 4

Page 138

(1) **b** Mass is measured in kilograms (kg).
  c Force is measured in newtons (N).
  d Frequency is measured in hertz (Hz).
  e Electric charge is measured in coulombs (C).

(2) Distance is measured in metres **(m)**.
Time is measured in seconds **(s)**.
Current is measured in amperes **(amps/A)**.
Temperature is measured in kelvin **(K)**.
Energy is measured in joule **(J)**.
Power is measured in watts **(W)**.
Pressure is measured in pascals **(Pa)**.
Electrical potential difference is measured in volts **(V)**.
Electrical resistance is measured in ohms **(Ω)**.

Page 139

(1) metres, kilograms, seconds
(2) C, Hz, kg, N, m, Pa, s
(3) **a** speed (metres per second, m/s) = $\dfrac{\text{distance (metre, m)}}{\text{time (seconds)}}$

  b wave speed (metres per second, m/s) = frequency (Hertz, Hz) × wavelength (metre, m)

  c electrical power (watts, W) = current (amps, A) × potential difference (volts, V)

Page 140

(1) **a** **i** 1.5 hours = 90 minutes
    ii 45 minutes = 0.75 hours
  b **i** 3 hours = 10 800 s
    ii 30 minutes = 1800 s
(2) **a** 2.6 kW = 2600 W
  b **i** 86 mm = 0.086 m
    ii 86 cm = 0.86 m

Page 141

(1) One measures current in A and the other in mA
(2) **a** 0 to 30 cm
  b because it is easier to convert from cm to the SI unit (metres, m).
(3) 60 + 51 + 0.63 = 111.63 s

Page 142

① Answer is 12mV not 12V

② a i Minutes have been used for time.

  ii The speed is given in km per hour, so the time must be in hours.

 b 15 minutes = $\frac{15}{60}$ hours = 0.25 hours

 c 50 km per hour × 0.25 hours = 12.5 km

Page 143

Exam-style question

1 Convert 50 g to 0.05 kg **(1)**

 KE = $\frac{1}{2}$ × 0.05 kg × 5^2 m/s **(1)**

  = 0.625 **(1)** J **(1)**

2 Charge (C) = current (A) × time (s) 0 s or Q = It **(1)**

 Convert 5 minutes to 300 s **(1)**

 Charge = 0.8 A × 300 s **(1)**

  = 240 C **(1)**

Page 144

Exam-style question

1 B

2 Rearrange to $I = \frac{P}{V}$ or current = $\frac{power}{voltage}$ **(1)**

 Convert 2 kW to 2000 W **(1)**

 $I = \frac{2000}{230}$ **(1)**

  = 8.7 A **(1)**

Unit 5

Page 146

① a i wave speed = frequency × wavelength

  ii $v = f\lambda$

 b i density = $\frac{mass}{volume}$

  ii $\rho = \frac{m}{V}$

 c i energy transferred = current × potential difference × time

  ii $E = I \times V \times t$

② a acceleration = a

 b current = I

 c density = ρ

 d frequency = f

 e force = F

 f kinetic energy = KE

 g potential difference = V

 h speed (or velocity) = v

 i volume = V

 j weight = W

③ acceleration = m/s²

 density = kg/m³

 spring constant = N/m

 wave speed = m/s

Page 147

① a i power, current and potential difference.

  ii power = current × potential difference

 b i power, energy and time

  ii power = $\frac{energy\ transformed}{time\ taken}$

② a resistance, current

 b power = current² × resistance

③ a energy transferred = charge moved × potential difference

  charge = current × time

 b charge = current × time

 c Because the question includes values for current and time.

Page 148

① a i

  ii current = voltage/resistance $I = \frac{V}{R}$

  iii resistance = voltage/curren $R = \frac{V}{I}$

 b i

  ii mass = density × volume $m = \rho \times V$

  iii volume = mass/density $V = \frac{m}{\rho}$

Page 149

① a distance (m), speed (m/s), time (minutes)

 b Convert time in minutes to seconds: 3 minutes = 180 s

 c distance travelled = speed × time

 d distance(m) = 20 m/s × 180 s = 3600m.

Page 150

Sample answer A:
- No conversion
- Wrong answer and no unit

Sample answer B:
- Acceleration has been squared; wrong answer

Sample answer C:
Working is correct but answer not calculated correctly

② force = mass × acceleration **(1)**

 500 g = 0.5 kg

 force = 0.5 kg × 10 m/s² **(1)**

  = 5 N **(2)**

Page 151

Exam-style question

① a start and end velocity (i.e. change in velocity), time

 b no

 c acceleration

 d need to include units: m/s²

② a acceleration = $\frac{change\ in\ velocity}{time}$

  or $a = \frac{v - u}{t}$ **(1)**

 b acceleration = $\frac{0 - 18}{3}$ **(1)**

 c acceleration = −6 m/s² **(2)**

③ energy transferred in stretching = 0.5 × spring constant × (extension)² **(1)**

 Convert 10 cm to 0.1 m **(1)**

 energy = 0.5 × 50 × (0.1)² **(1)**

  = 0.25 (J) **(1)**

Page 152

Exam-style question

1 C **(1)**

2 a force = mass × acceleration **(1)**

 b rearrange to acceleration = $\frac{force}{mass}$ **(1)**

  $a = \frac{12N}{0.5\ kg}$ **(1)**

  = 24 m/s² **(1)**

Unit 6

Page 154

(1) Any variable that can be measured, e.g. current, force, temperature, mass, potential difference, energy, resistance, power, length, speed, acceleration, etc.

(2)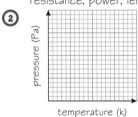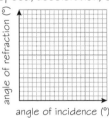

Page 155

(1) a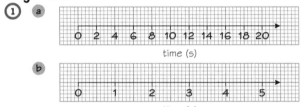

b

(2) a Each small square on the horizontal scale represents 0.2

b Each small square on the vertical scale represents 2

(3)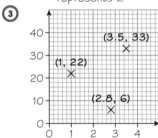

Page 156

(1) a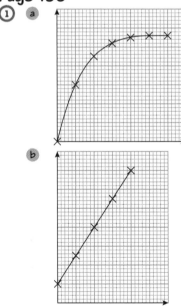

b

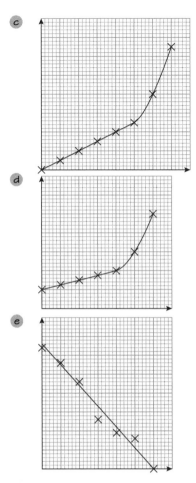

Page 157

(1) a As the time increases, the velocity decreases. As it is a straight line this is a linear relationship. As the gradient is constant, the velocity decreases at a constant rate.

b At first as the potential difference increases the current is zero (or very low). It then reaches a value (0.3V) when the current suddenly increases sharply as the voltage increases, and the line goes up very steeply.

Page 158

(1) a Errors are: no units on axes; tram lines (double lines); dot-to-dot rather than a smooth curve.

b Errors are: the graph has not used half of each axis; points are not evenly distributed above and below the line of best fit, so this is not a good line of best fit; there are no scales on the axes; the axes have not been labelled.

c Errors are: the scale on the x-axis is wrong (10 has been missed out); the label and unit are missing from the x-axis

Page 159

Exam-style question

(1) a potential difference

b current

c Marks will be gained for:
- Axes with linear scales that use more than half of each edge of the grid and are labelled with units from table **(1)**
- All points correctly plotted to ± half a square **(1)**
- A single straight line passing through all points and the origin **(1)**

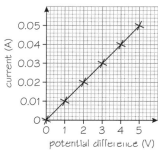

(2) The current is directly proportional to the potential difference (as there is a straight line through the origin). The gradient is positive and constant so the current increases at a constant rate.

Page 160

Exam-style question

1 a

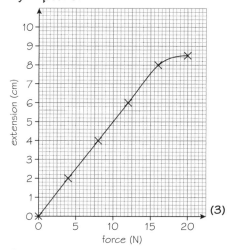

(3)

b As the force increases, the extension increases. From 0 to 1.6N the graph is a straight line through the origin, showing that extension is directly proportional to force. (1)

For forces greater than 1.6N the graph is a curve, which gradually gets less steep. This shows that the extension is still increasing, but more and more slowly. (1)

Unit 7
Page 162

(1) a explain
b compare and contrast
c assess
d describe
e compare

Page 163

(1) Compare: give similarities and/or differences between the three types of radiation in terms of the properties given

(2) Three – alpha, beta and gamma

(3) range in air, ability to penetrate through materials, ability to ionise atoms

(4) a Explain
b how the energy stored in the ball changes as it is through up into the air and comes back down again; calculations
c 0.2 kg, 4 m/s, $g = 10$ N/kg

Page 164

Beta radiation – key information underlined Beta particles (β^- or $_{-1}^{0}e$) are high speed electrons with high energy. Beta particles are <u>moderately ionising</u> and can <u>penetrate further</u> into materials. They can <u>travel a few metres in air</u>. They have a relative

mass of $\frac{1}{1835}$ and a charge of -1. They are <u>stopped by aluminium a few millimetres thick</u>.

- range in air? a few metres
- ability to penetrate through materials? stopped by a few mm of aluminium
- ability to ionise atoms? moderately ionising

Gamma radiation – key information underlined

Gamma rays (γ) are high frequency electromagnetic waves. They are <u>weakly ionising</u> and can <u>penetrate materials easily</u>. They can <u>travel a few kilometres in air</u>. They need <u>thick lead or several metres of concrete</u> to stop them. They travel at the speed of light.

- range in air? a few kilometres
- ability to penetrate through materials? only stopped by thick lead or several metres of concrete so very penetrating
- ability to ionise atoms? weakly ionising

Page 165

(1) a shortest; only; less than
b Example answer: Beta radiation has a longer range in air than alpha radiation and can travel a few metres. It is stopped by a few mm of aluminium so penetrates more than alpha radiation. It is not as good as alpha radiation at ionising atoms.

(2) a only; whereas; However; furthest
b Alpha radiation has the lowest penetration through materials and is stopped by a sheet of paper. Beta radiation can penetrate further and is stopped by a sheet of aluminium a few millimetres thick. Gamma radiation has the highest penetrating ability and is only stopped by thick lead or several metres of concrete.

Page 166

(1) Following phrases should be crossed out: 'Alpha radiation is alpha particles that are helium nuclei which contain two protons and two neutrons and have a relative mass of 4.' and 'Beta radiation is high speed electrons with a charge of −1.'

(2)

	alpha	beta	gamma
range in air	✓	✓	✓
penetration	✓	✓	✓
ionising ability	✓	✗	✓

(3) No - the student has compared range and penetration for all three, but has only compared the ionisation of alpha and gamma.

(4) It would make more sense to write the paragraphs in the order alpha, beta, gamma and to write the properties for each one in the order given in the question.

(5) Student's own answer.

Page 167

(1) a Assess – carefully consider all the relevant factors and choose which are the most important. Then come to, and write, a conclusion.
b Student's own answer.
c Student's own answer.

(2) Here is part of a sample mark scheme for the question. Some sample answers are included to help you understand it. Your teacher will be able to show you examples of complete mark schemes.

The indicative content below is not prescriptive and candidates are not required to include all the material which is indicated as relevant. Additional content included in the response must be scientific and relevant. **AO2 (6 marks)**

diesel – fossil fuel made from oil; non-renewable/will run out; store a lot of energy; easy to store and use in engines; releases CO_2 when burnt; contributes to climate change/global warming; emits particulates; causes air pollution/breathing difficulties;

bio-fuel – renewable/won't run out; made from animal waste or plants; can be made from wood or uneaten plant material; some crops grown specifically for bio-fuel; releases CO_2 when burnt; carbon neutral; same amount of CO_2 absorbed during photosynthesis as released during burning; energy still required to produce the fuel so not really carbon neutral; uses land space which could be used for food production; can increase food prices relevant conclusion given

Level 1 (1–2 marks)

This would be given if two or three of the factors are given for one or both fuels but with no conclusion or scientific links.

Level 2 (3–4 marks)

This would be given for stating factors about both fuels including some scientific links e.g. diesel is a fossil fuel so contributes to global warming when it is burnt as it releases CO_2.

Level 3 (5–6 marks)

This would be given for stating factors about both fuels including scientific links and a conclusion as to the suitability of the fuels e.g. Despite it's contribution to global warming, diesel is the better fuel to use as it is more readily available; or Even though it uses large amounts of land, bio-fuel is a more suitable fuel as it has less impact on climate change. There is no right or wrong conclusion, it is what you decide and support with scientific evidence.

(3) Student's own answers.

Page 168

Exam-style question

Command word is 'explain' so some reasoning needs to be given, e.g. how the energy is transferred as the speed decreases (KE decreases) and the height increases (GPE increases).

Suggested answers for each level.

Level 1 (1–2 marks)

Basic statements about kinetic and/or gravitational potential energy (GPE) without any linked detail.

Level 2 (3–4 marks)

Maximum kinetic energy when it leaves her hand, transfers to maximum GPE at the top of the throw. As ball comes down, GPE is transferred back to KE. The speed the ball is thrown at has an effect on the amount of kinetic energy and hence the amount of GPE and height the ball goes.

Level 3 (5–6 marks)

Include at least one calculation.

Use of $KE = \frac{1}{2}mv^2$ to calculate the initial energy as the ball moves up. [$0.5 \times 0.2 \times 4 \times 4 = 1.6\,J$]

Maximum GPE is 1.6 J, height reached by ball = Δh =

GPE $\frac{GPE}{mg} = \frac{1.6}{0.2 \times 10} = 0.8\,m$